Carving Santa and Mrs. Claus

Ken Blomquist

*Text written with and photography by **Jeffrey B. Snyder***

Schiffer Publishing Ltd

4880 Lower Valley Road, Atglen, PA 19310 USA

Contents

Library of Congress Control Number: 2002114578

Designed by Mark David Bowyer
Type set in Windsor BT/Aldine 721 BT

ISBN: 0-7643-1765-2
Printed in China

Published by Schiffer Publishing Ltd.
4880 Lower Valley Road
Atglen, PA 19310
Phone: (610) 593-1777; Fax: (610) 593-2002
E-mail: Schifferbk@aol.com
Please visit our web site catalog at **www.schifferbooks.com**
We are always looking for people to write books on new and related subjects. If you have an idea for a book please contact us at the above address.

This book may be purchased from the publisher.
Include $3.95 for shipping.
Please try your bookstore first.
You may write for a free catalog.

In Europe, Schiffer books are distributed by
Bushwood Books
6 Marksbury Ave.
Kew Gardens
Surrey TW9 4JF England
Phone: 44 (0)20-8392-8585
Fax: 44 (0)20-8392-9876
E-mail: Bushwd@aol.com
Free postage in the UK. Europe: air mail at cost

Acknowledgments

I want to thank some very special people for making this book possible. My own Mrs. Claus, my wife Mary, and daughter Kate, my #1 elf, have given me the inspiration to carve a new Santa each year. Bill Veasey gave me the knowledge to do more than just carve. Yolanda Presberry turned my stick figures into patterns. My shop elf, Bill Horner, enables me to produce enough Santas each year to supply my collectors.

Special thanks to my editor, Jeff Snyder, and publishers, Peter and Nancy Schiffer, for their patience, help, and encouragement.

Introduction

I began carving my series of Santas in 1990. Each year I choose a different country and do extensive research before coming up with my design. For this book, I have chosen the familiar American Santa introduced in 1822 when Clement Moore wrote "A Visit of St. Nicholas." Political cartoonist, Thomas Nast, used Moore's description of St. Nick as the basis for his illustrations of Santa in *Harper's Weekly* from 1864-1886. It was in 1931 that artist Haddon Sundbloom created ads for the Coca Cola Company that first pictured the fat, jolly, red suited Santa we see everywhere today.

Because Santa needs someone to make sure everything is done by December 24, I'll show you how to carve Mrs. Claus as well.

Tools and Supplies

band saw with 1/4" skip tooth blade (4tpi)
square
hot glue gun and glue sticks
flexible shaft machine with:
- carbide bits
- steel cutters
- carving stones

carving knife and leather strop
small carving chisels
dividers
propane torch or kitchen mini torch
tin snips
wood-burning pen
nylon scrubby pad or fine wire brush

Note—You do not need every tool on this list to complete the projects. If you don't have a band saw, or just want to save time, I have blanks available that can be completed with just a carving knife. These blanks come in basswood, tupelo gum, white pine, sugar pine, or white cedar.

Note—if you plan to texture the carving as I do, choose a wood with a pronounced grain.

Paints
lacquer base sanding sealer
flat white spray paint
red gesso
white gesso
Acrylic paints in:
- alizarine crimson (red)
- titanium white
- iridescent white
- Cerulean blue
- Mars black
- Prussian blue
- burnt umber
- gold
- heavy body white
- Hooker's green dark
- flesh tones—light and dark (craft paints are fine for faces)

MinWax™ Early American oil base stain

Brushes
1 inch wash brush
1/2 inch wash brush
#8 round brush
liner brush
stylus

Miscellaneous Supplies
brass or copper shim stock for cookie tray
24-26 gauge wire for glasses
1/2 teaspoon applesauce
1 teaspoon cinnamon
white glue

To Make Mrs. Claus's Cookies

Mix 1 teaspoon cinnamon with a 1/2 teaspoon applesauce. Add 1/8 teaspoon white glue. Knead with fingers 'til smooth. Roll out with pill bottle or magic marker and cut out with a sharp knife, tiny cookie or aspic cutters. Dry on a paper towel or rack 'til hard.

Hints and Suggestions

- After you cut out your pattern, glue it to tag board to make it sturdier.
- Use a photocopier to reduce the pattern to make a necklace or enlarge it for a larger carving. You may want to use plywood and just cut out a silhouette.
- Use hot glue to keep your profiles together.
- Use slightly larger stock for your first cut out, then you can use the left over material as a pattern.
- If your wood has a knot or other imperfection, you can use auto body putty as fill or as a glue to repair. If you are very careful, as soon as your putty begins to dry, you can cut it with a knife. You won't have much time, so pay attention.
- Consider Mr. and Mrs. Santa as the first two pieces in a rather elaborate chess set. A red and green chessboard would make a great gift.
- Don't be afraid to change the facial features (especially the mustache) or clothing colors. Historically, Santa has not always been dressed in red and white.
- Round over the back of your band saw blade. Doing so will enable you to back out of your cuts. (Of course your industrial arts teacher told you never to do this!)
- Nibble with your band saw blade when cutting out your patterns. Take your time—it will save time later.
- Always use sharp tools and good quality paints and brushes.
- Let your paint set up for a few days before using the oil based stain.
- Make sure you start with square stock.
- Once you have laid out your Santa with centerlines, do not remove the centerlines while doing your initial rough out.
- Clean out your carbide bits and sharpen your knife often. Use your strop.
- Wear a leather apron and a facemask, especially when grinding off material. You will create a lot of sawdust.
- Wear safety glasses and turn on your dust collector.
- If you don't have a dust collector, set up a box fan in front of you, put a furnace filter on the back, and set it to blow away from you.

Project One:
Mrs. Claus

The most important part of your carving begins when you lay out and cut out your pattern properly. Take your time with both of these procedures. Make sure the pattern is in line with the grain of the wood. Another major consideration is the wood you plan to use. The wood you use will determine the finish. Eastern White Cedar is my personal preference. Our finished Mrs. Claus will be made from Eastern White Cedar. White pine is adequate, as are sugar pine, basswood, and tupelo gum. Cut your stock to 8" long x 4" x 3". Cutting your block a little oversized doesn't hurt as you can use the leftovers for wooden patterns. It helps to have your stock as square as possible. You get a better pattern with square stock. A joiner and table saw or band saw work well to square your stock.

Once we've made sure that our stock is square, we want to use a square to align our pattern.

We want to have a square profile to align both the front and side patterns.

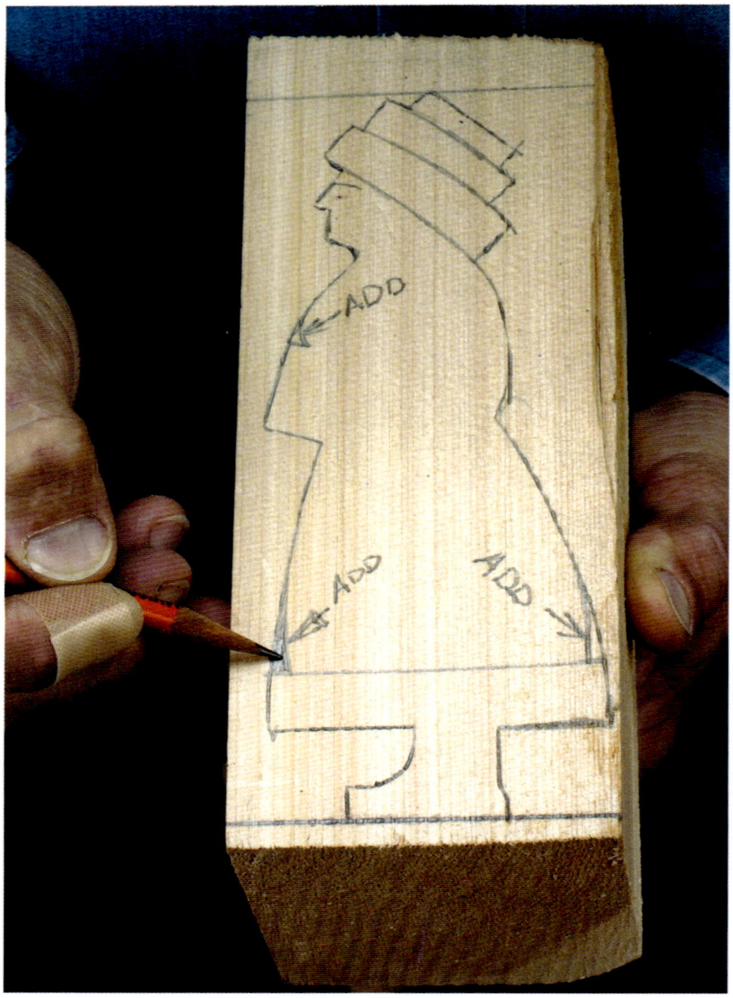

My band saw blade suggestion is a 1/4", skip tooth, 4 teeth per inch (tpi) saw blade. It is not necessary to worry about the detail around the fur. The shaded area shows material added to make your cut out easier. You will cut the front profile first. When you begin, take your time. This cut is important in your pattern development.

Before you cut, however, take a stone and round over the back of your blade very gently. That makes backing out of your cut much easier.

Begin to cut along the pattern lines. As you make your cut, try your very best to leave the lines. If you cut outside the line or inside the line, don't worry. Remember, you're cutting out hair, fur, and cloth, none of which are perfect.

Take your time and nibble away at the extra material between the feet with the saw blade.

Like so. Sliding the stock back and forth against the blade cleans out any extra wood. This area is very difficult to get to later. Cut out your profile. Save the shell. To do this takes some time but is well worth it in the end.

The front profile has been cut. Cut what you can accurately. You can separate the profile from the shell and go back and make any detail cuts that you couldn't get on your original cut out. Nibble away stock in the corners when you have to.

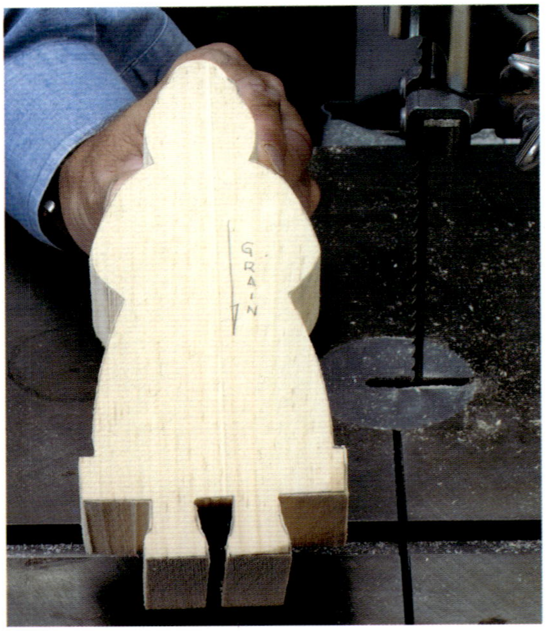

You could begin your carving from here, with just the front profile; …

The side profile has been cut. If your stock or band saw are not perfectly squared, you will get some incomplete cuts.

however, I prefer to cut the side profile. Again, this is going to take some time, but it will save you a lot of work. There are a number of ways to attach the cut out stock to the shell. You can use rubber bands, tape, or brads. I like to use hot glue. Please do not use too much glue, just enough to hold. Apply your hot glue to the areas outside the pattern, as shown here. Caution: too much glue applied inside the pattern lines will gum up the saw blade as it passes through.

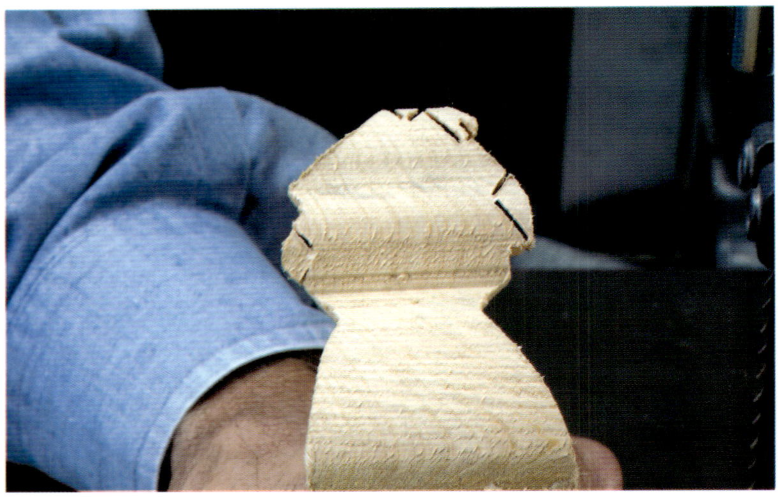

Clean any incomplete cuts up with your carving knife.

If you have laid out your pattern on large enough stock, you can trim off a thin slice with the band saw for future use as patterns, both front and side. Go back and clean up these patterns once cut. A little trimming and sanding will give you a clean pattern with some permanence for repeated use.

Take the time to add reference lines on all four sides. This helps to establish your carving to round. Reference lines should be approximately 1/4" away from either side of center.

Lay out both the oval of the skirt and the shape of the boots on the base of the carving.

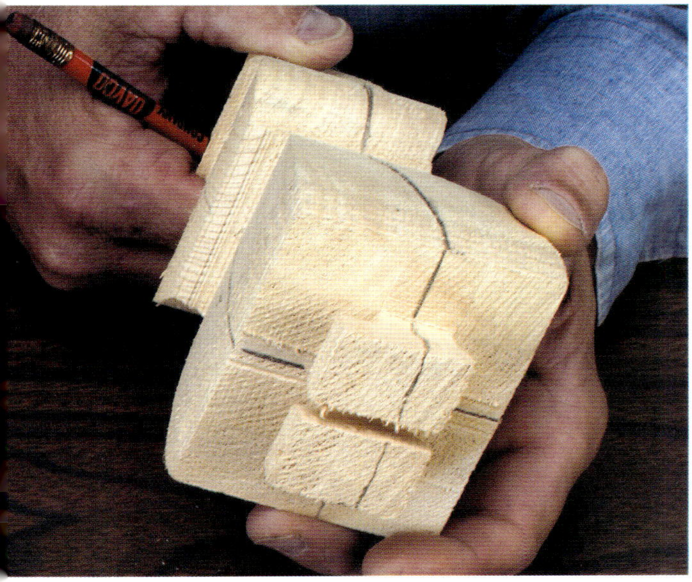

Add centerlines all the way around the body on all four sides, including the bottom. These lines do not have to be perfect. Like horseshoes, close is good.

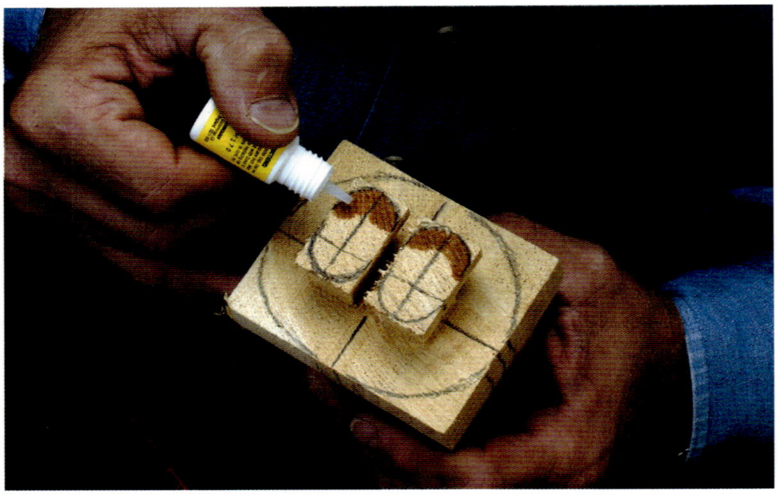

Add some Super Glue™ to the boot tips to strengthen them. This way, if you drop the carving, the boots are less likely to break.

I use a #6 Knotts™ knife, one well worn and one brand new. Take the time to sharpen your knife before you start. I'm using a leather strop treated with aluminum oxide and oil (3-in-1™ or WD-40™ both work well).

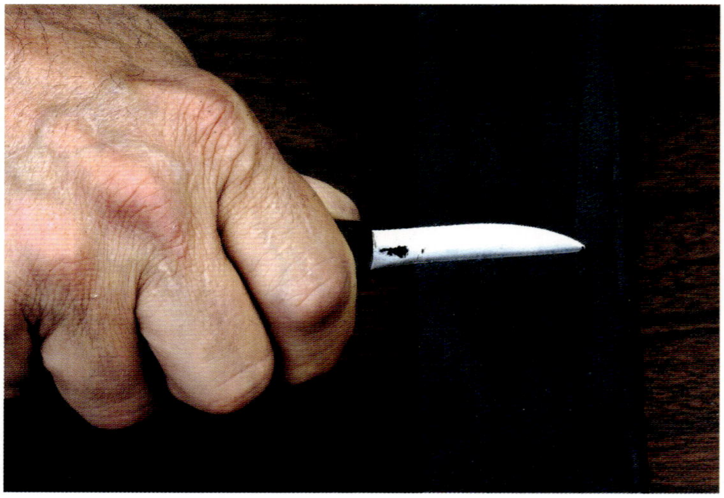

I keep my knife blade flat on the strop, moving it back and forth over the surface an equal number of times on both sides. I usually strop my knife about every half hour while I'm carving.

We'll start rounding Mrs. Claus from the skirt up, from reference line to reference line. Begin rounding the skirt. Leave the reference lines and the line on the bottom in place. Do not remove them at this time.

Here are our first cuts.

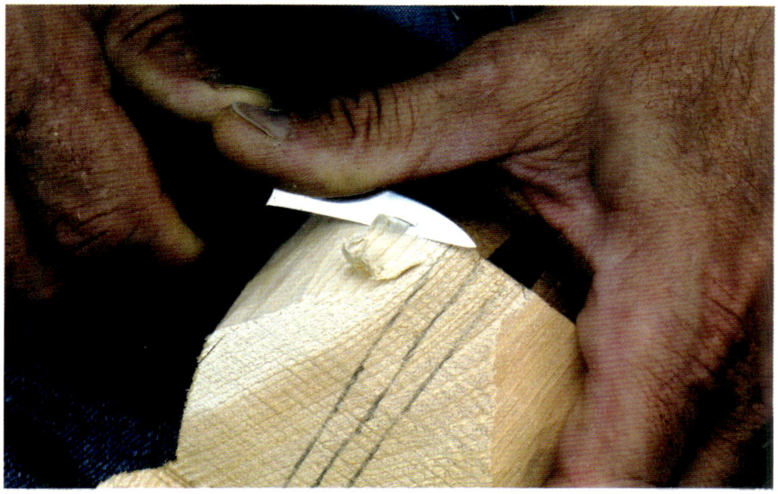

If you come across an irregularity in the grain, you may need to reverse your cut to prevent the wood from chipping out.

Add the fur line. You have the option to add fur or not, if you want to make this a straight skirt without fur across the base, that is fine.

Round off the boots in the same manner.

The skirt is rounded and the reference lines are left in place. This is a preliminary rounding of the skirt. We will go back later and round again.

Now round up the arms, chest, and back.

The body is rounded.

Moving on to the head, round as before.

If you do not have the equipment to properly round down your block or do not wish to go to all that effort, there is another option. You can purchase a rounded down Mrs. Claus blank from me.

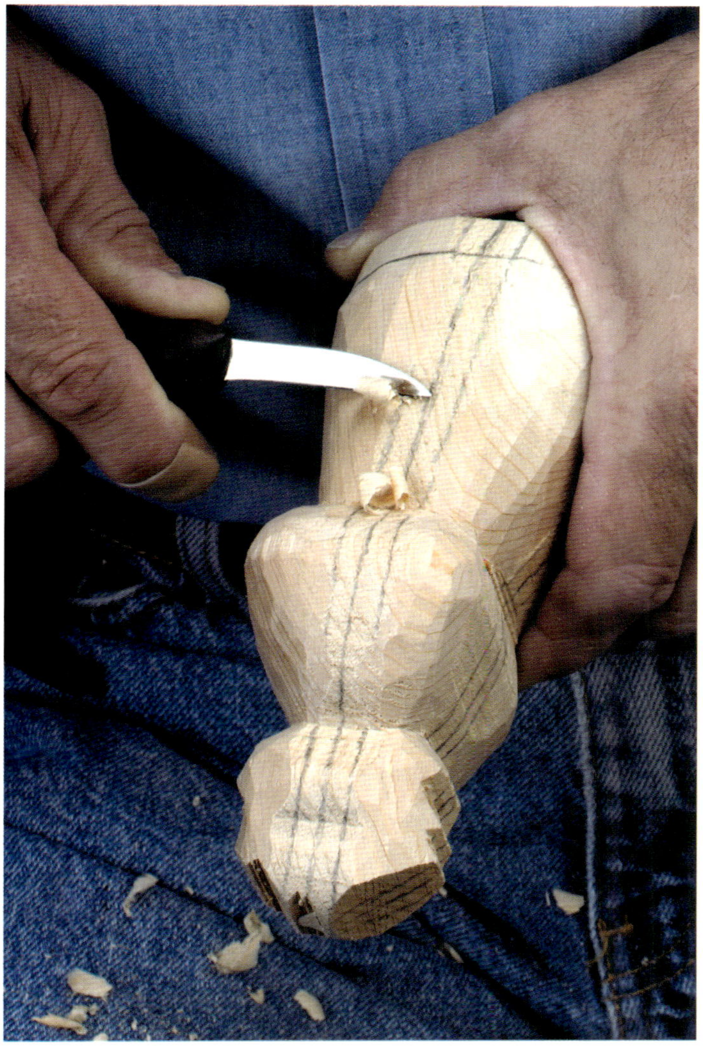

Now use your carving knife to remove the reference lines, keeping the body round. Leave the centerlines in place.

It is time to cut in the fur at the base of the skirt. Make a deep cut straight into the fur line.

Reduce the wood of the skirt above the edge of the fur cut line to make the fur stand up away from the skirt. Because we added extra material to our pattern, it doesn't hurt to take the centerline away.

Now that you have defined the fur, you need to remove the ridge that you have created part way up the skirt, shaping the skirt into the waist.

The skirt is shaped. You can be as creative as you want with the shape of the skirt. You can leave it very round or make it more fitted.

We're going to start to carve away the area between the mittens. Do this by making a V cut from each mitten into the waist. Begin by scoring a deep line on center.

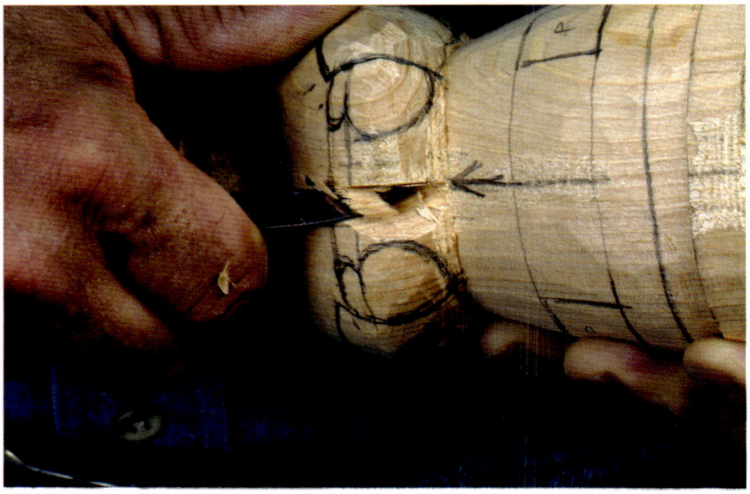

Start to cut from the mittens to the centerline, making a V cut.

Even though you are not going to use all of these new reference lines now, it is a good idea to lay out the apron, mittens, arms, hair line, and hat line. If you would like to add pockets to the apron, lay them out now. It's an option.

The V cut is in place.

We need to remove additional area from between the mittens up into the chest. Make two V cuts along the sides at 45 degrees from the center.

Define the mittens, removing material up to the cut lines.

Like so.

It is important that you back cut from the top of the mitten to the chest at a slight angle. We are going to cut in under the mitten a bit.

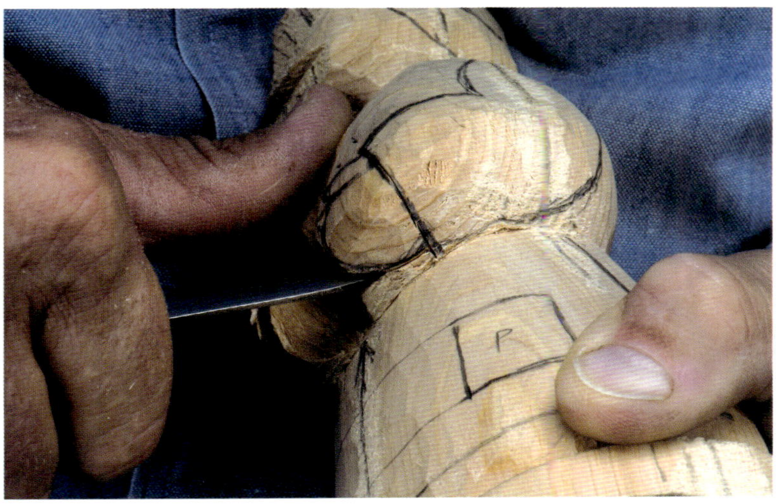

Score around the mittens, including the cuff.

We are going to score along the arm lines from the cuff into the elbow and the elbow into the shoulder. This cut needs to be fairly deep because you have a lot of wood to take out. Don't try to make your cut all at once, make several passes in order to get about a 1/4" depth. The deepest part of the cut (1/4") needs to be at the elbow. Don't cut quite as deep at the shoulder.

The extra material has been removed from both arms, upper and lower.

Start to relieve the material on the chest to the forearm.

At this point, start to round over the arms, round over the mittens, and define the mitten from the sleeve. The arm is rounded.

The extra material has been removed from the forearm and upper arm. You are now beginning to form the arms, chest, and neck.

Back cut from the mitten into the sleeve about 1/8".

Continue to round over the mitten. While rounding, we need a V cut at the thumb line.

The mitten is rounded.

Come off the skirt with the knife up into the upper body to create a waistline. Lay the knife on the skirt and cut up into the upper body between the mittens to create that waistline.

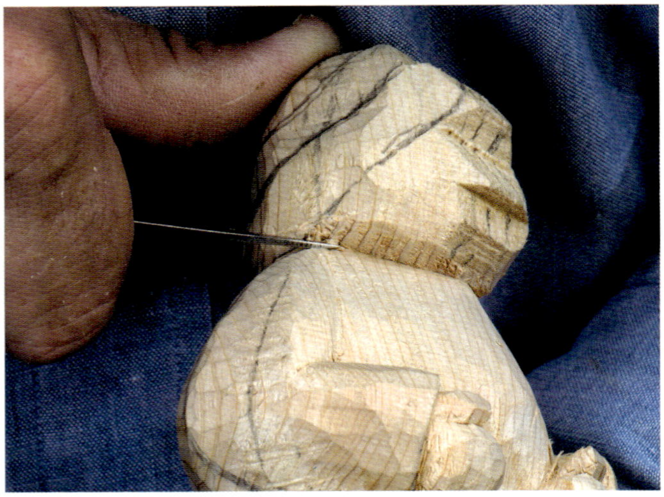

Begin to define the neck and head. Make a fairly simple cut up into the neck.

I'm now cutting from the upper body down to the waist.

After establishing some of the neckline, we establish the hairline. Score the hairline with a fairly deep cut.

The waistline is in place. Take some time to form the chest and the top of the skirt into the waist. The shape of Mrs. Claus's waist and chest is a matter of personal taste. At this point you should have the waist, chest, mittens, and arms shaped.

Now, cut from the face up into the hair.

Round out the face a bit. Round from the cheek up to the hairline and the cheek down to the chin.

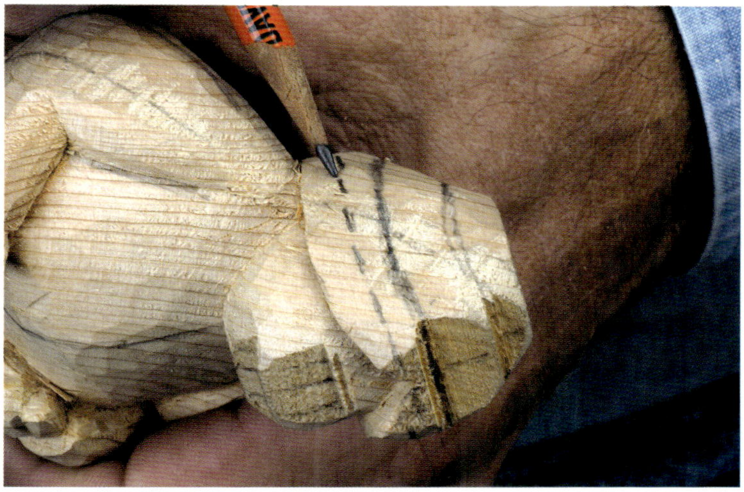

The face is rounded.

Shape the lower part of the hair into the face and into her back. Do this by rounding off from the centerline down. The centerline here is the dashed line.

I've done some rounding in the back on her hair, shoulders, and back.

Looking from the top of her head down, you will probably have some corners to round away.

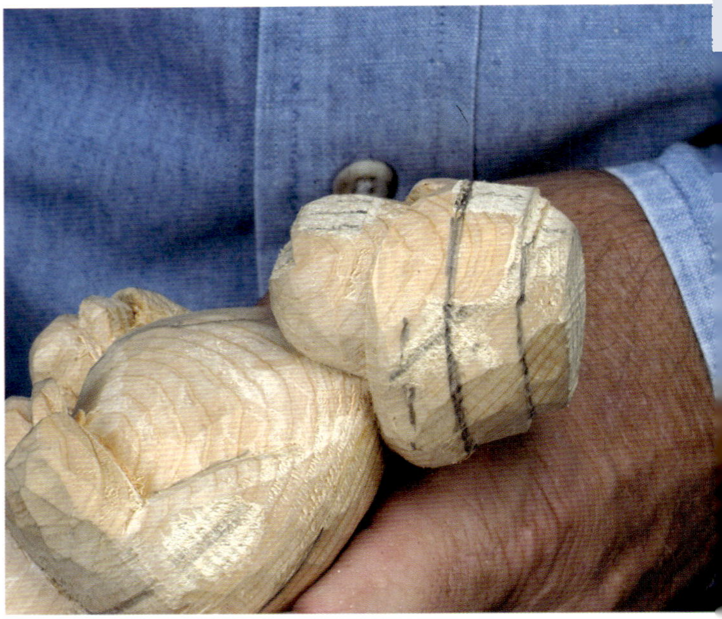

Redraw your reference lines and define the hat and the hair.

Score the line between the hat and hair.

The corners have been rounded.

Once the line has been scored, there is a fair amount of hat that must be carved away. There is about 1/8" to 3/16" worth of excess wood to be carved away.

Round over the hair into the hat.

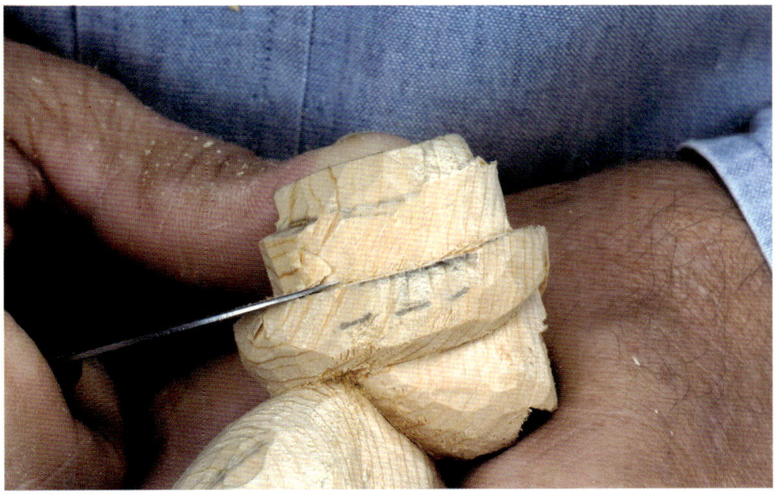

The hat is rounded.

Draw in the reference line for the upper portion of the hat again and score that line.

Take away the excess wood from the top of the hat

We have defined the fur and the top of the hat. Now we will round over both the fur and the top of the hat, just as we did with the hair.

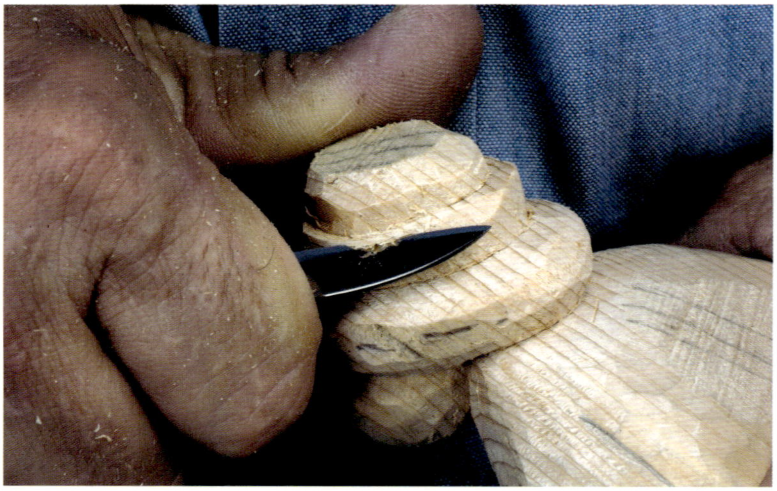

Rounding the fur.

I'm making a little scoop cut in the top of the hat to get rid of the saw marks and reference lines.

The fur and the top of the hat are now rounded over.

Moving on to the face, first lay in the details of the nose. I've noticed that the hairline might be a bit too high and I may decide to change it later.

The area around the face is always a bit of a problem to score with a knife. I like to use a wood-burning pen to score the lines of the face. It is just a little easier.

Once the lines were burned in, I traced over them to make sure I had an even score. Carve away the excess wood on either side of the nose. I have decided to change the hairline and I am also reestablishing it. Remove the material from the side of the nose. From what would be the high point of the cheek, round down toward the chin, out to the ear, and up to the hair.

Removing material from the other side of the nose.

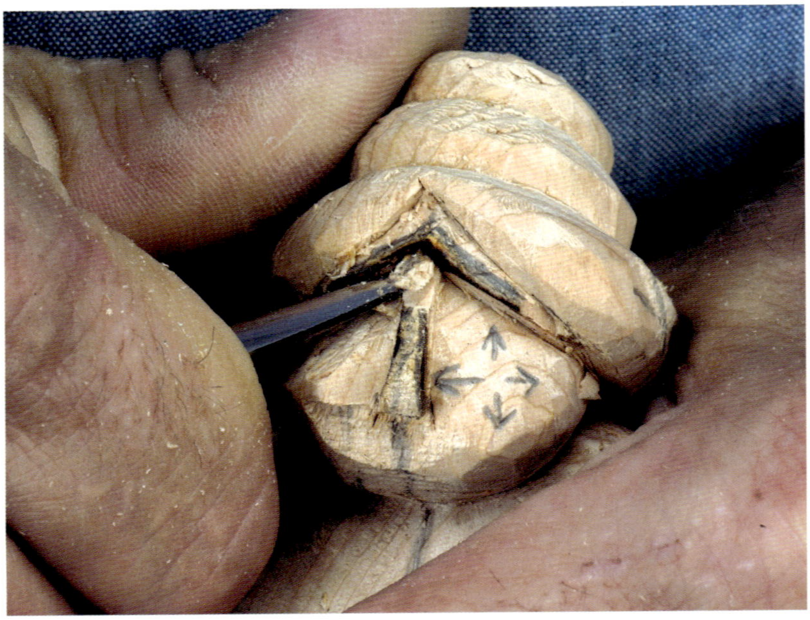

Remove excess material from the bridge of the nose as well.

I'm going back and fixing the hairline, lowering it a bit. I redrew a lower hairline, scored it with the burner, and am now reshaping the hair into the face and the hat, until I get the look I want. I am able to do this because the original pattern was somewhat oversized.

The face is rounded.

Round over the top of the nose. I leave the nose slightly exaggerated due to the type of finish I use on my Santas. The reason for this will be come apparent later.

The new hairline is established.

The hairline has now been redone to my satisfaction. It is important to remove the old score lines.

As you'll notice in the previous pictures, I've left a lot of material in the face area. The face is the hardest part of this carving. That is why I've given you so much wood to work with. You need to take some time and shape the face both from the front and side profile. Facial structure is a matter of taste. Round from both the front and sides.

I've drawn in the placement of the eyes and the mouth. I've also added the facial structure of the cheeks on either side of the mouth.

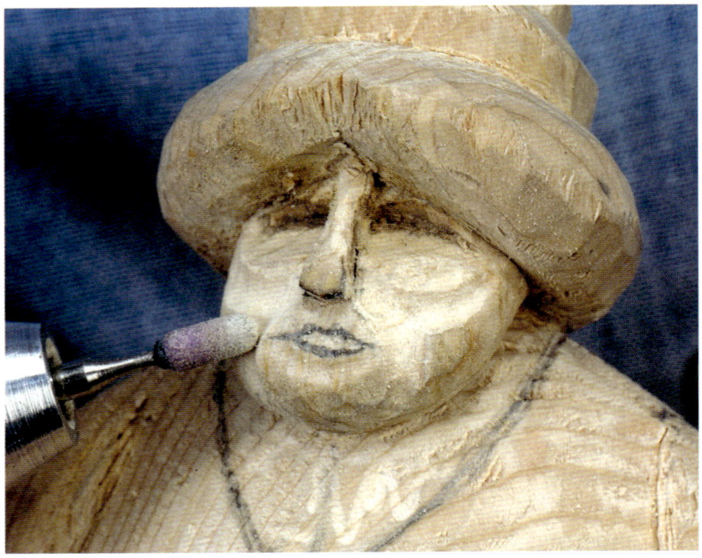

Use the mini-grinder to cut in the lines around the mouth and cheek. I don't like to use a knife for this job. It is difficult to get an indentation that is not a sharp line with a knife. The mini-grinder with the round stone is better for this job.

There are a number of ways to cut in the eyes. You can use a small grinder, a knife, or a chisel. I prefer to burn in the brow and make a V cut with my knife.

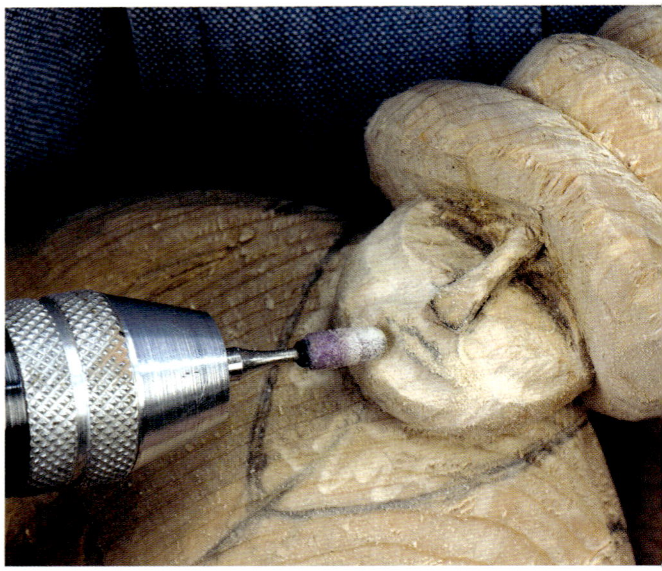

Use the same stone to form the underside of the bottom lip and the chin, cutting in an indentation to create both of these features.

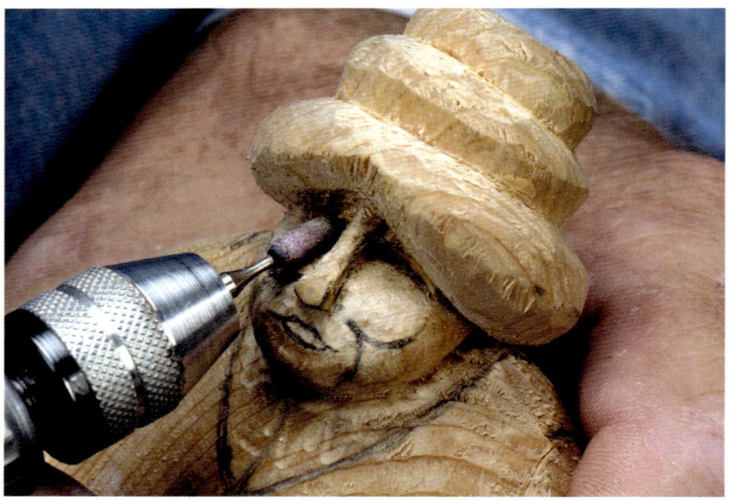

I like to use a round stone on my mini-grinder to clean up the inside of the eye.

Take the same stone and round over all of the ridges you formed when you made your indentations. Try to keep the mouth drawn in to give you some sense of proper placement while you work. There needs to be some exaggeration in the face. The way I texture my carvings requires a little extra material.

So far, we have done very little work on her back. Now is the time to move around and form the arms. Scoop out the back of the arm with a carving knife and a scoop.

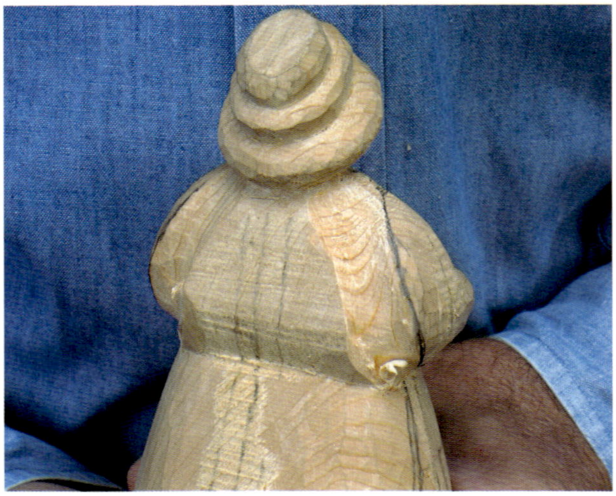

The back of the arm is in place.

The back and arms are rounded.

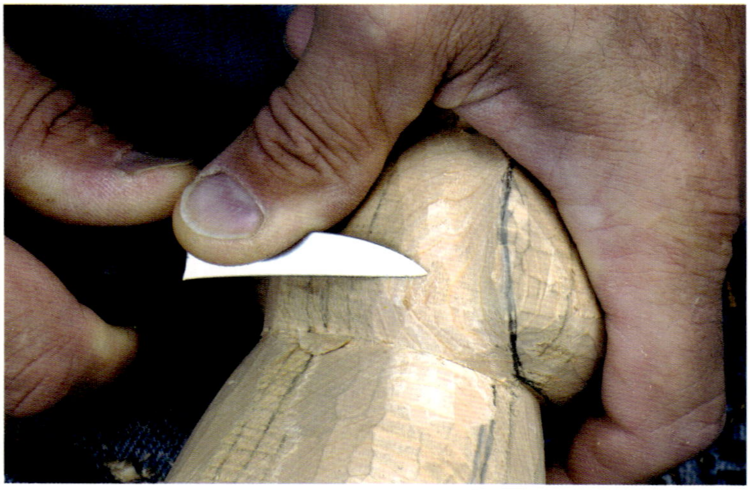

Round over the back and the arms.

We need to work on her waistline and finish forming the elbow and the back of the arm.

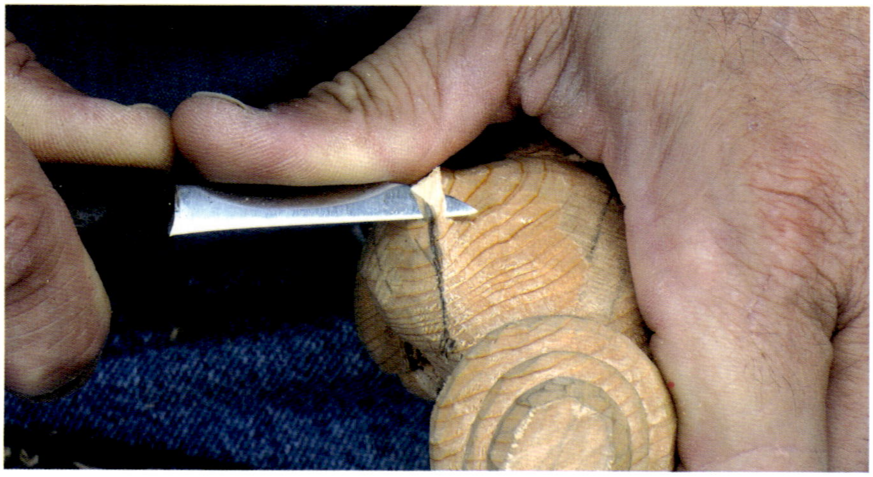

Rounding over the arm.

One side is now finished. The pencil lines show what remains to be done.

Details

The basic features of the figure are now in place. There are a number of details that must be added to finish Mrs. Claus. The first thing to do is to round off the fur at the bottom of the skirt. You may need to cut some of the skirt away to create more fur.

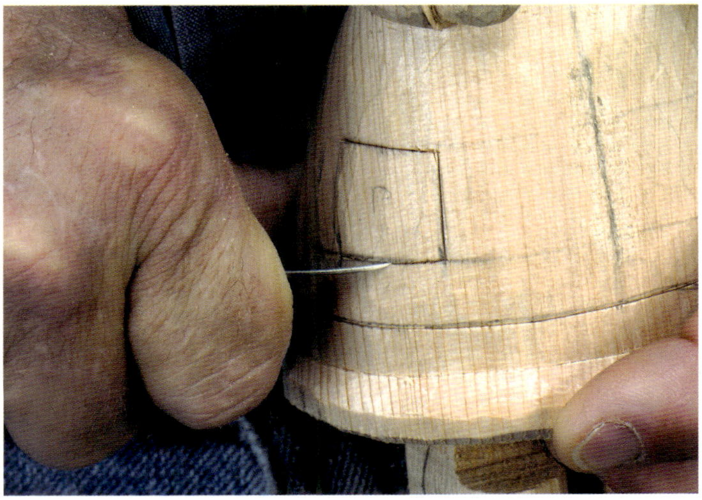

Mrs. Claus comes with an apron. Score the lines on the apron and the apron's pockets with your knife now.

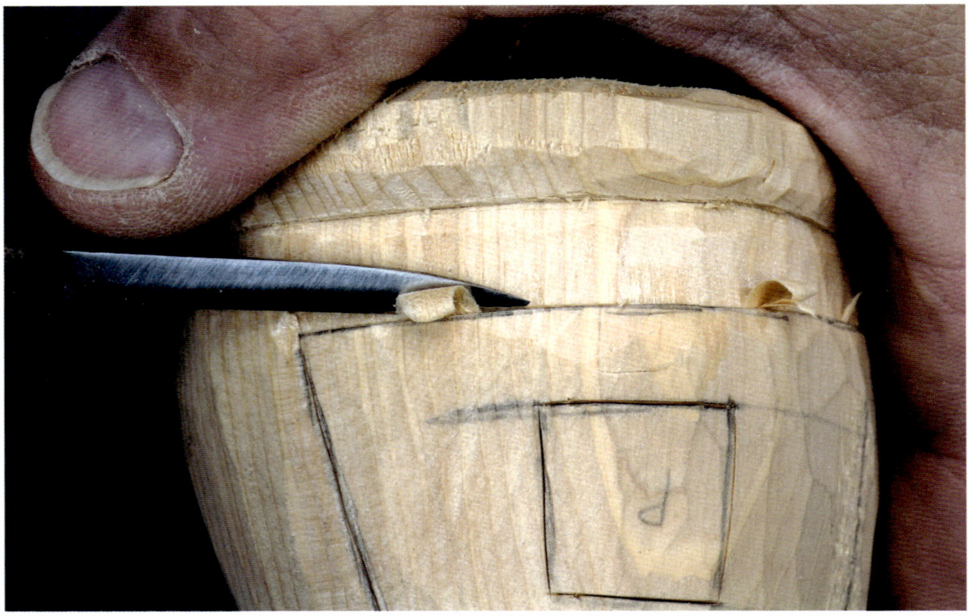

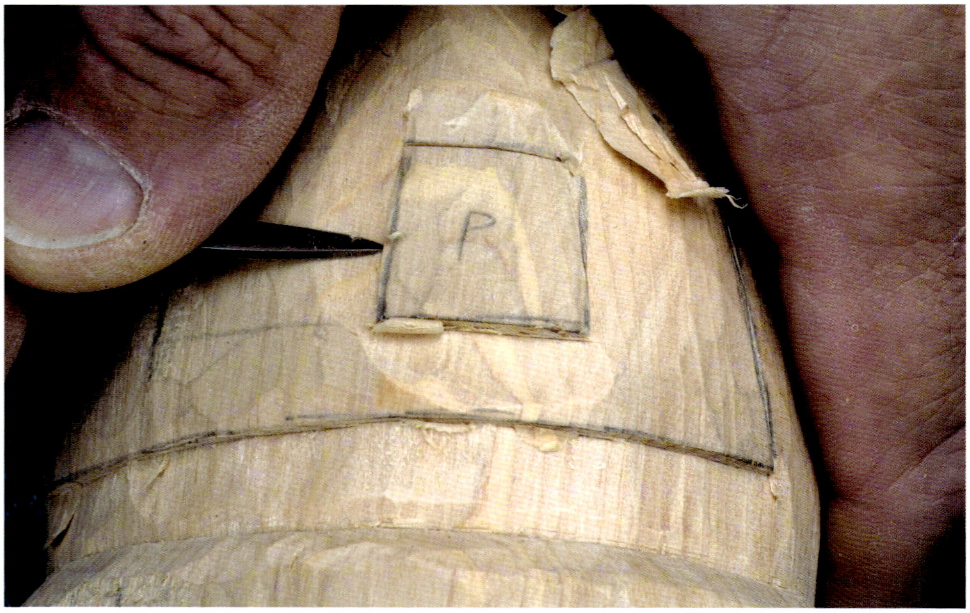

Back cut to the apron and the pocket score lines.

The details around the bottom of the apron and the pockets are finished. Notice that I have left the cuts a little thicker than you might expect. Now we need to move on to her upper body.

Draw in the shape of the top of the apron.

This is a difficult area to carve because of the way the grain runs and the very tight space you have to work with. I've chosen to relieve the apron away from the blouse. You may want to paint it in rather than going to the effort of relieving this area.

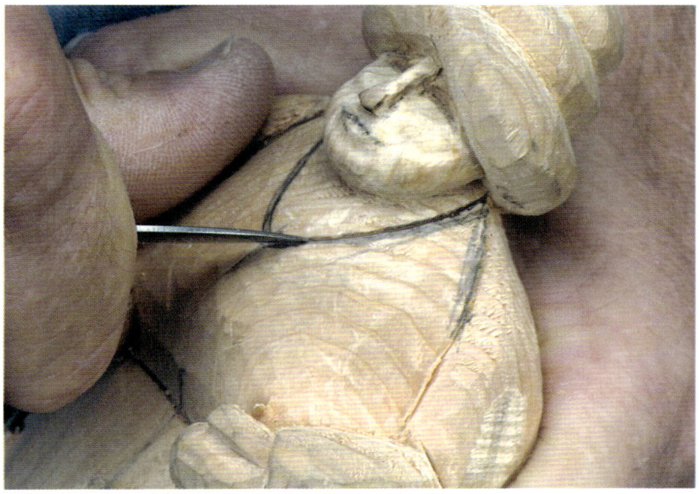

Scoring the lines of the apron.

The apron is now in place.

Relieve wood away from the outside of the apron.

Draw in some crease lines at the elbows and the waist (front and back).

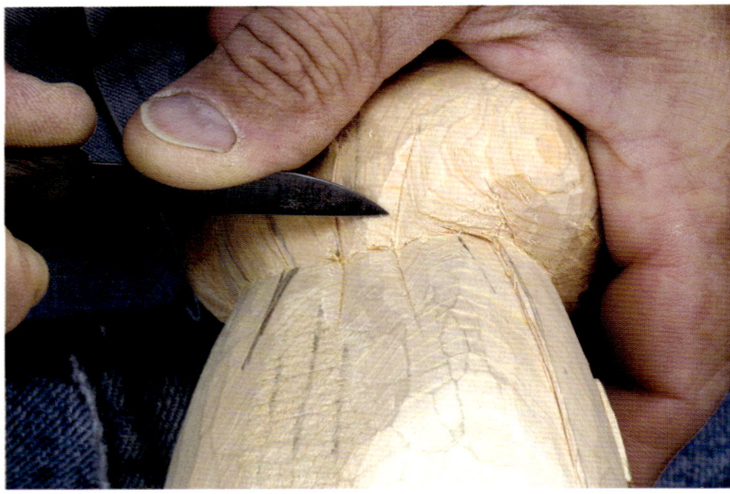

Cut the crease in with a V cut. When you cut in the crease line, we want to start light at the far end of the crease and end heavy at the center of the crease line, in this case where the crease meets the waistline.

Score each crease line.

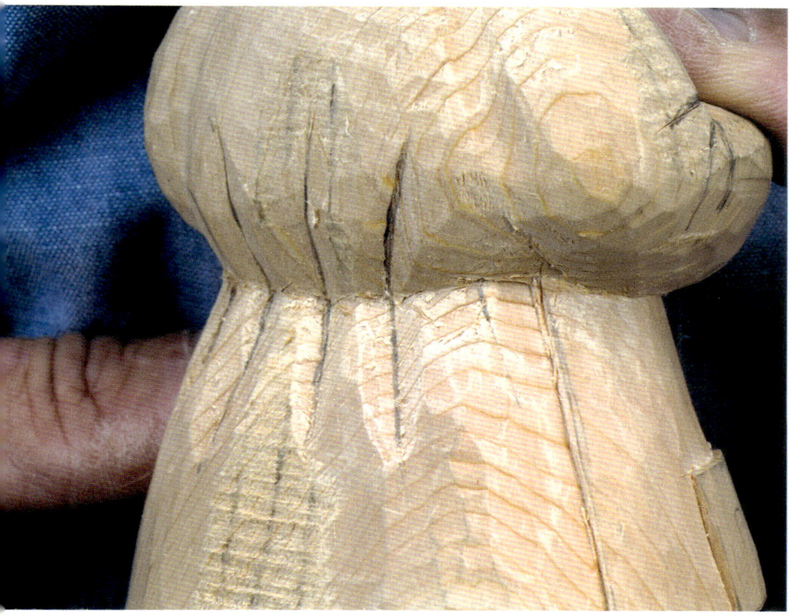

All of the creases along the back are in place. I have added pencil lines here to help show the depth of the crease. You do not need to add these pencil lines yourself! The elbow and front waist creases are now in place. There are a number of ways to put in these creases. If you have a good V chisel, you may want to use that. You may want to use a burning pen to score the creases and then cut them in. You may want more or less, the choices are yours.

Moving on to the boots. This is the final bit of carving. First, redefine the boots and make sure that they are the same size. Then, carve in the boots and straighten them up. Keep them a little oversized so that Mrs. Claus has a broad base to stand on. First round off the back of the heel. The heel in the foreground has been rounded down.

Go around to the front of the boot and round off the corners at the top and front.

Round over the toe of the boot.

The boots now have their basic shape. You have a chance to do a number of things at this point. You can now leave the boots as is or dress them up a bit with soles and heels. Draw in the sole and heel. We'll save laces for Santa himself.

Because the boot is a relatively small area, and difficult to get to, I'm going to score the lines of the sole with my wood-burning pen. Once they are burned in, relieve the shoe away from the sole. The sole should be a little larger than the shoe. Be careful cutting here as you are cutting with the grain and it is easy to take off too much. The soles are now in place.

With the heels, just make a slight back cut from half way down the sole to the heel line. This can be a somewhat difficult cut.

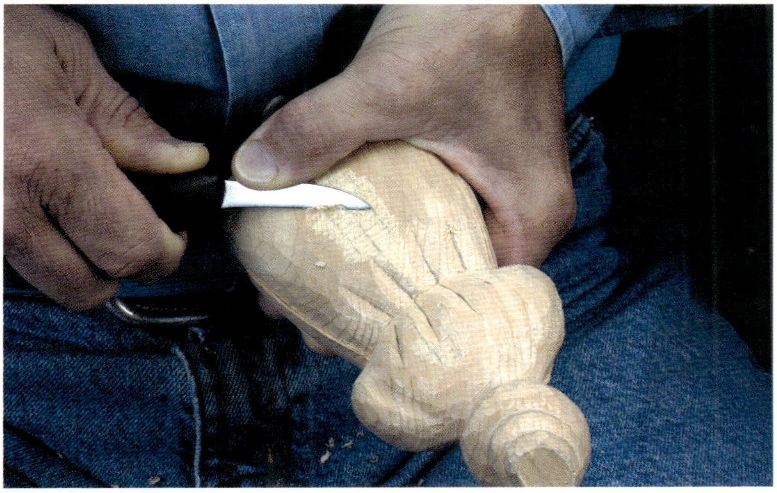

Now that the majority of the carving is done, you need to get rid of saw lines and all your pencil lines. You also need to balance the figure and clean up the cut lines and edges. You need to do as much cleaning as possible as there will be no sanding of this figure.

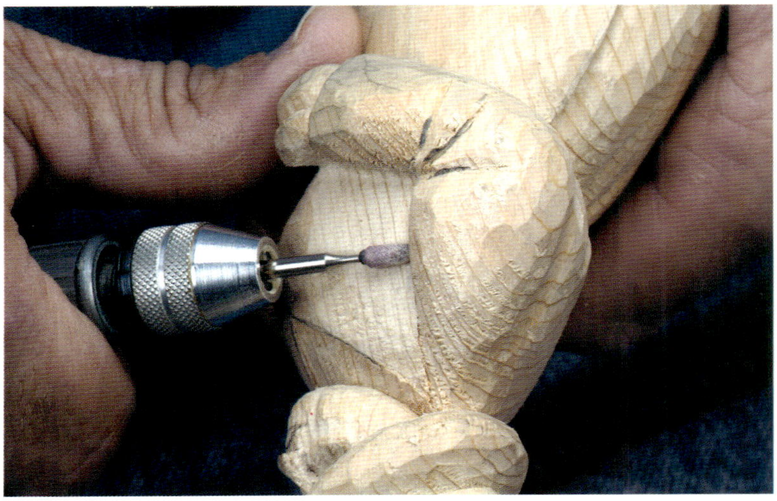

As a last step, I take a stone and go over all of the corners, edges, and rough spots to clean up a bit.

Mrs. Claus is carved, cleaned, and ready for texture.

Texturing Mrs. Claus

The next step is not for the faint of heart. To achieve the appearance of aged wood, I use a burning torch ... very carefully ... playing the flame lightly over the entire carving. This blackens the surface of the wood. You may want to experiment on some scrap wood first.

To clean up your carving, I suggest you use a toothbrush on the face. You can also use a *very soft* wire brush and clean with the grain. Try your best not to clean across the grain. Sometimes that is not possible, but try to go back and do some cleaning with the grain.

When I burn, I always burn on the thicker parts and edges first. I hold the carving by the head and burn the fur, apron, and lower skirt first. My suggestion is to wear a leather glove on the hand that holds the carving and use a bare hand for the torch (which gives more control of the torch). Burn a little at a time. Do not let any of your wood glow or catch flame. Put any burning points on the carving out immediately. My suggestion is to wear a leather apron and smother any flames on the figure against the apron front. When I switch the carving to burn the top, I usually use a small kitchen torch. It has a smaller flame and is easier to control. Try your best not to put the flame directly on the face. You should get enough peripheral burning to blacken the face without distorting the features.

To clean the rest of Mrs. Claus, I use a kitchen scrubbing pad mounted on a flexible shaft tool. Once again, you need to clean with the grain. You may notice that your carving has checked, you may have uneven burning, you may have lost some detail, or you may find some "unusual" features in the wood you didn't know you had (I found a bullet once!). I like to call all these things "patina." Leave them in place. It will make your carving your own. As I said, you are probably going to lose some detail during texturing. That is why we exaggerated the features earlier in the carving process. Depending on how much you lose, you may need to go back and touch up your carving.

I used a "test" cookie tray to line up the burn lines in her mittens where the actual tray will slide in place. I use a very thin brass, copper, or tin shim stock for my cookie trays. You can also make your tray from wood.

Painting Mrs. Claus

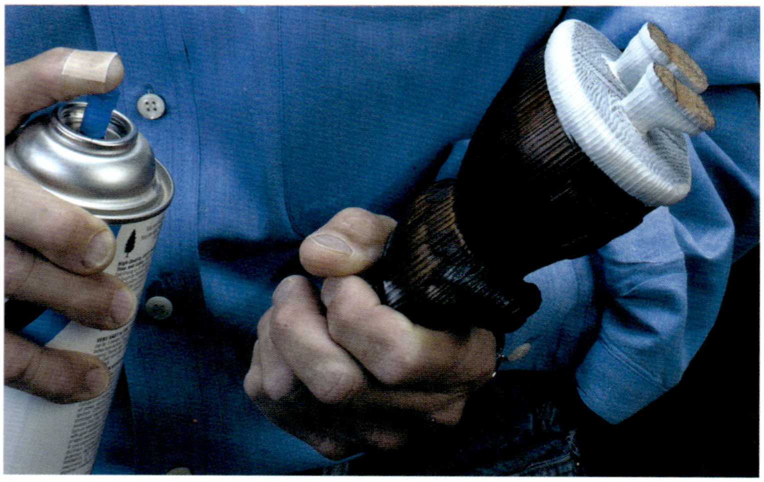

Once your carving is clean of *all* charcoal, it's a good idea to wipe it down with a clean rag or a paper towel. Make sure you don't have any little bits of cloth, towel, or cleaning pad left in the surface and seal the figure with a good lacquer or lacquer based sanding sealer (or both). You may notice that I am a step ahead. I've put some white primer on the fur.

The amount of pressure used will determine how clean Mrs. Claus becomes. If enough pressure is applied, you can take the wood almost back to its natural state

Apply the base coat of white on the fur. HINT: if you are interested in spraying your paint on, use a good, flat white multi-purpose paint (gloss white is very difficult to paint over). I use plumber's tape to mask off around the area I want to paint. Remove the tape as soon as possible.

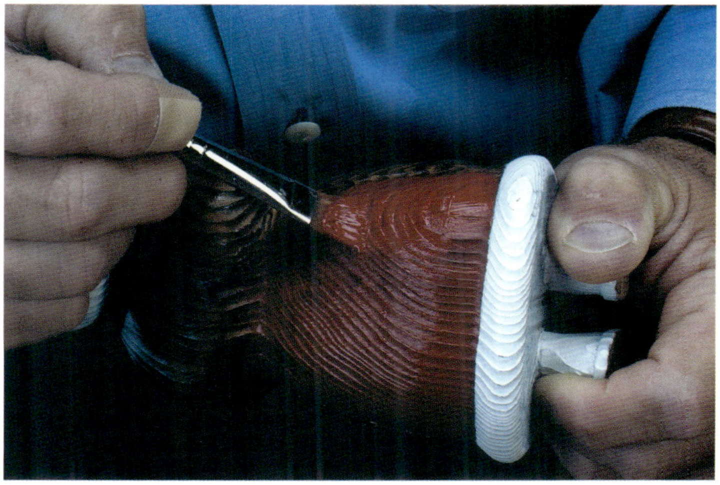

Paint the dress with a good quality red gesso. I use a small, flat wash brush to apply the paint.

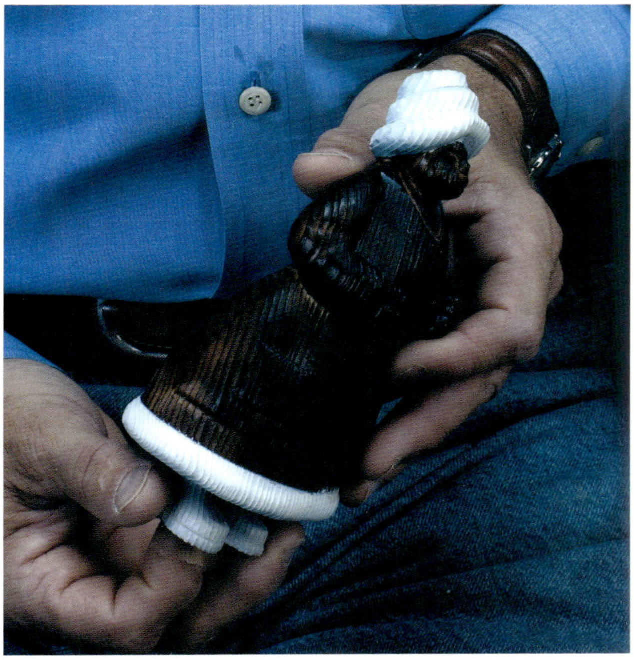

In this picture you can see that I have sprayed the hair and fur of the hat along with the fur at the bottom of the skirt ... and the boots.

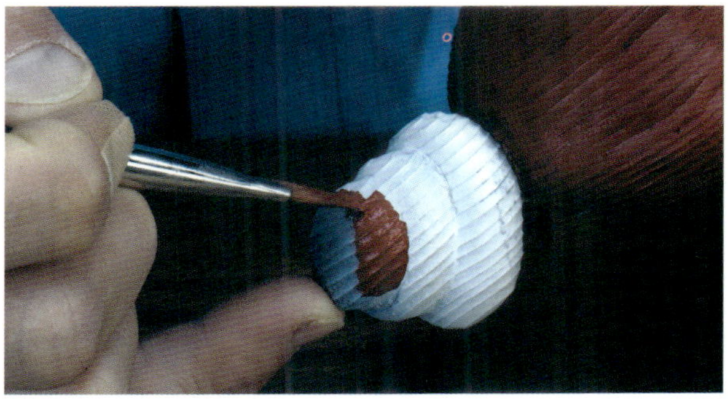

Moving on to paint the top of the hat: when putting your red gesso over white, the white is a little harder to cover. Whatever color you decide to use over the burnt wood, that color will come out darker. Greens or purples will come out nearly black, at least a shade or two darker than comes out of the tube.

You can use a hair dryer to hasten the drying time of your paint. However, please do not use your dryer on its highest setting *and* never dry the sanding sealer with a hair dryer. Sanding sealer needs to dry naturally.

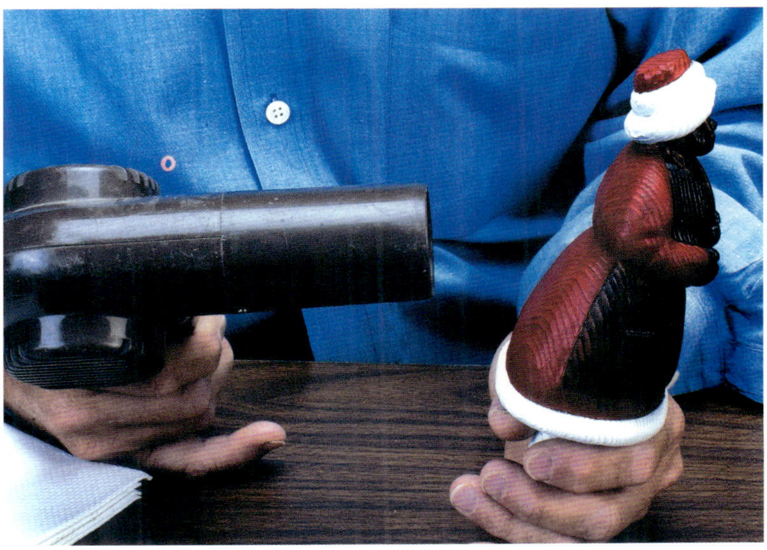

Don't forget the front of Mrs. Claus's dress above the apron line!

The red is now in place ... with one exception.

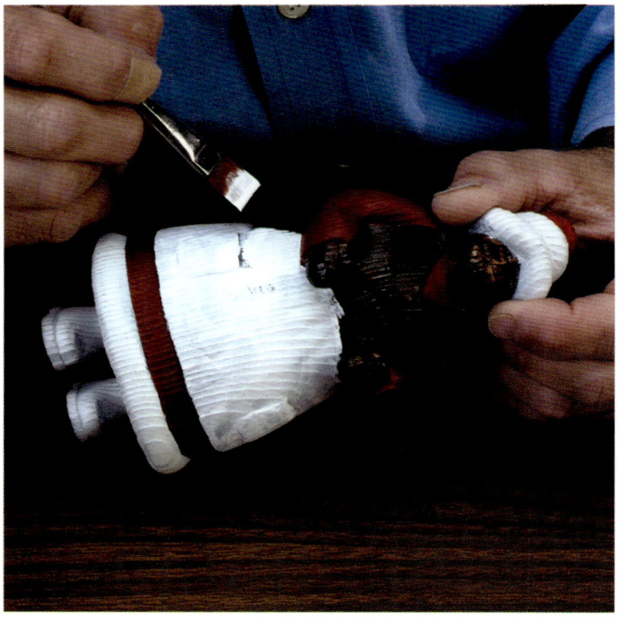

Use white gesso on the apron, face, and mittens. I've had several requests for African-American Santas in the past, so what I've done is leave the face natural following the texturing and cleaning, which creates a beautiful dark skin tone. Painting the apron, I always paint from an edge toward center. I try to put the paint on as evenly as possible. It is not always easy, but it is worth a try.

If you used spray paint, use the white gesso to touch up any areas that you could not reach with the spray, such as under the hair. The white is now applied to the apron, mittens, and face.

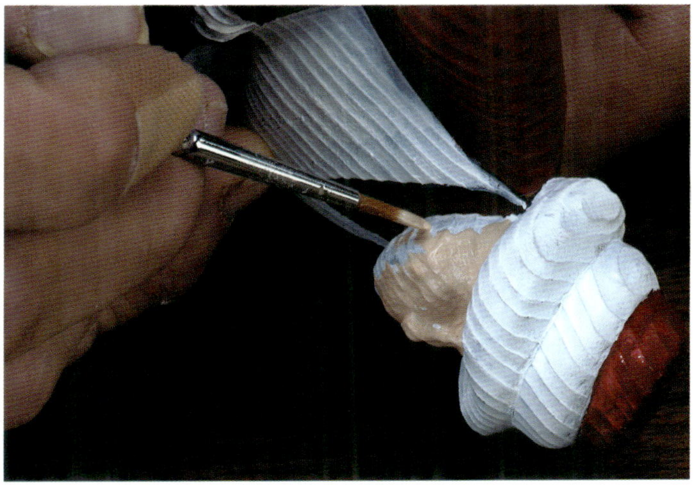

If you want to turn the mittens into hands, this is a good time to apply flesh tone there as well. However, since my Mrs. Claus is carrying a hot cookie sheet, she needs the mittens. Here, I am applying flesh tone to the face.

The flesh tone is applied to the face.

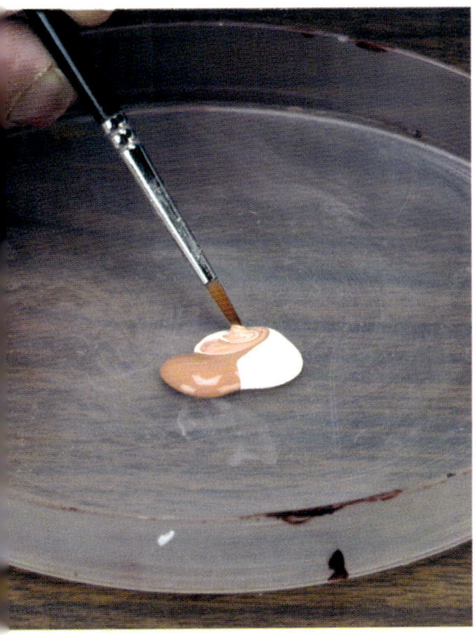

Paint the face with a mixture of light and dark flesh tones. Choice of skin tone is up to you.

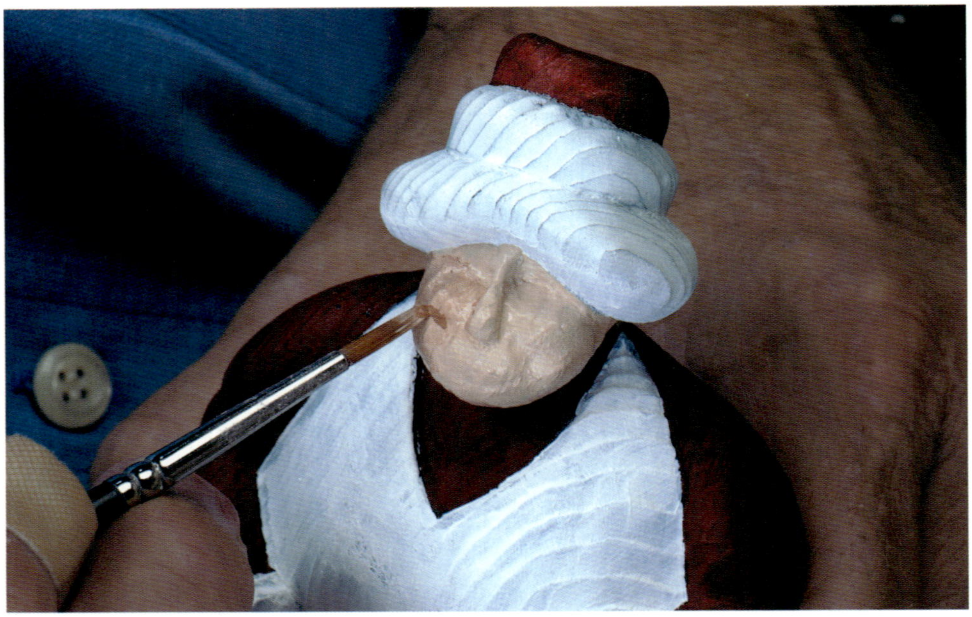

Take some of the darker flesh tone, using a wet brush, and swirl this color in to the applied flesh tone. Mix this in to create some shading.

Mrs. Claus now has all of her basic coats of paint. I'm going to apply some black gesso to the boots. The color of the boots, however, is completely up to you. You can use brown, black, or leave them white.

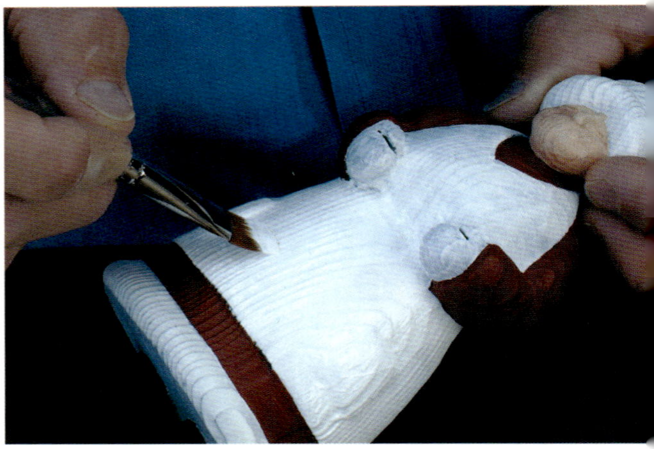

Applying a final coat of white on the apron (there are many whites on the market to choose from). I am using a coat of titanium white, applied fairly wet and thin. Should you get white paint on the red, take a clean, wet brush and wipe it off right away. It may take a couple strokes, but it will get the white paint off. If you lost any detail in burning, you can go back and paint it in now.

For the final coat of paint on the red, there are any numbers of reds on the market. I use permanent Alizarine Crimson for my final coat of red on Mrs. Claus. Try to limit the number of coats of paint applied so as not to lose the grain we worked so hard to show.

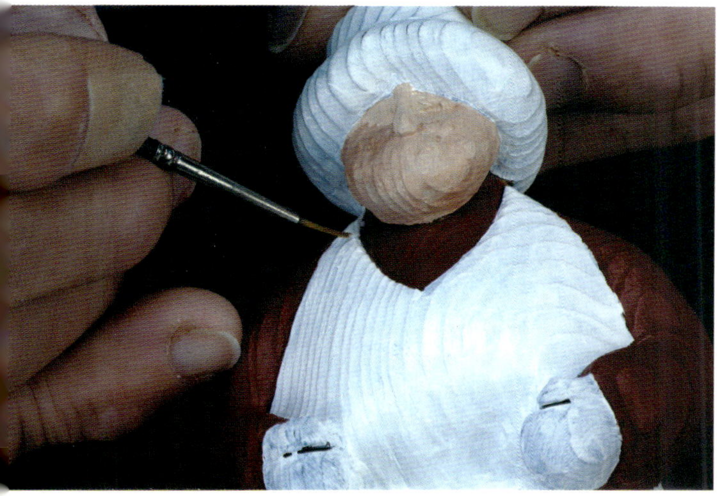

For instance, I lost a little detail on one side of the apron and am widening that side with the white paint.

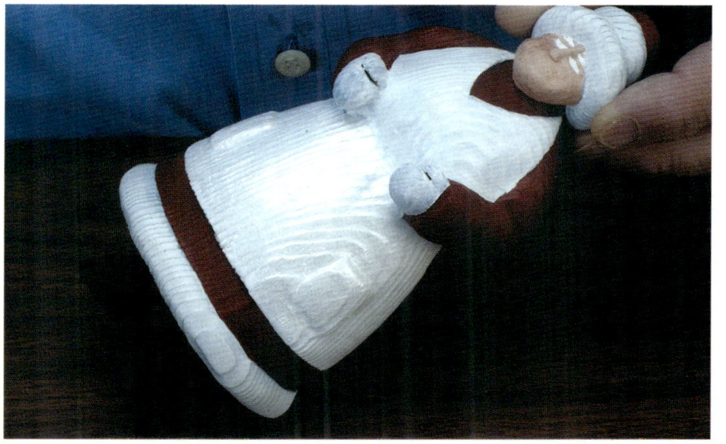

To simulate an old-fashioned oilcloth apron, I'm using a wash of iridescent white as a final coat. While the iridescence will not cover another color, it does create a pleasing effect. The bottom half of the apron has the iridescent white coat in place in this photo.

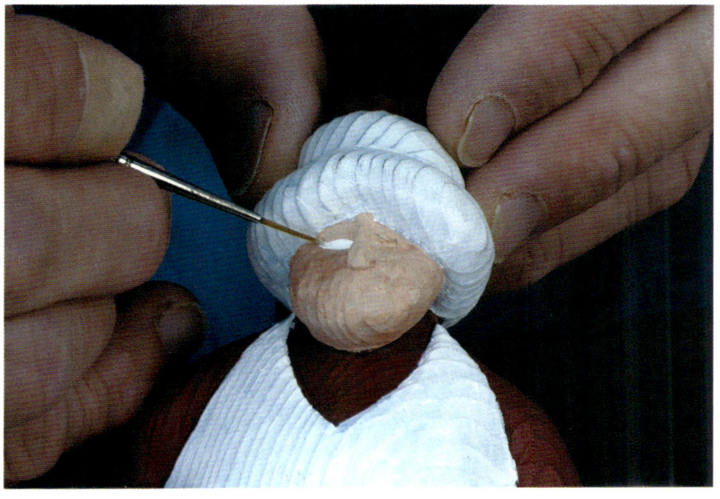

While you have the titanium white paint out (or if you are using gloss white on the apron), take a liner brush and paint in the eyebrows and the whites of the eyes.

The final coat is now in place on the apron.

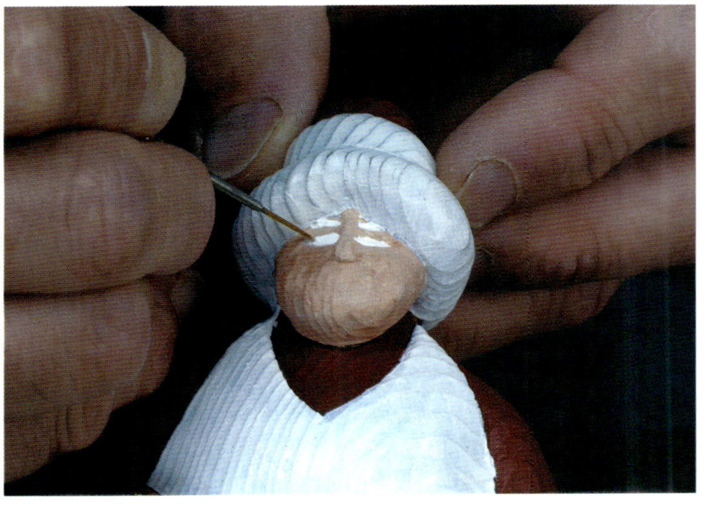

The whites of the eyes and eyebrows are painted in. She doesn't look very happy yet, does she?

Add a heavy bodied acrylic paint (I use titanium white) to the fur on the hat, dress, and mittens. I apply it with a sponge. This gives a textured look, enhancing the fur.

The textured fur is applied. When you finish the hat, you might want to use the small brush to add a tiny bit of texture to the eyebrows.

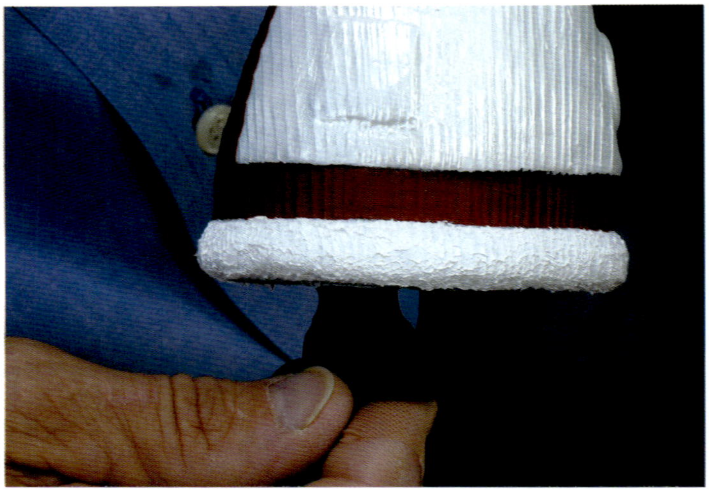

The titanium white is now applied to the fur at the base of the dress.

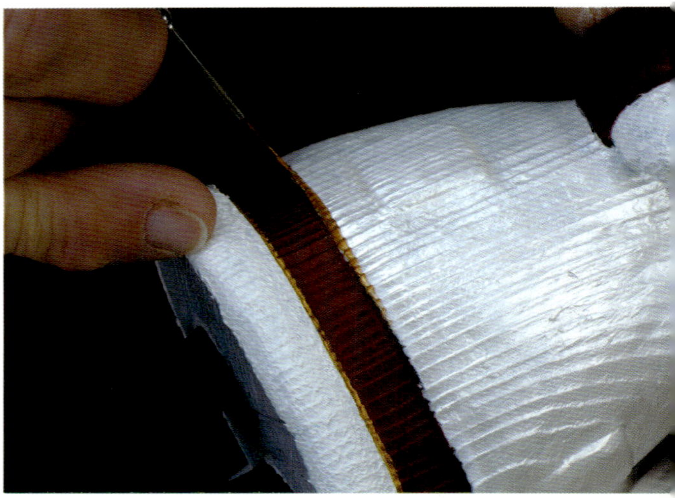

Add some gold accent around the fur, the apron, and the hat with a liner brush. You will not get a perfect pinstripe-straight line because of the raised grain. You can make the accent lines any color you wish. I prefer gold.

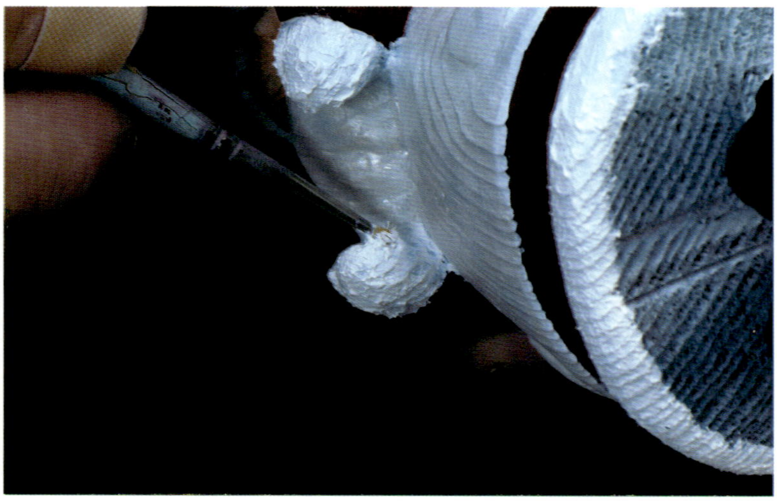

For hard to reach spaces, cut off an old paintbrush to use in place of the sponge. Remember that this is supposed to be fur: it does not need to cover completely and can come up a little onto the red of the dress as fur would. Dry each section before you move on.

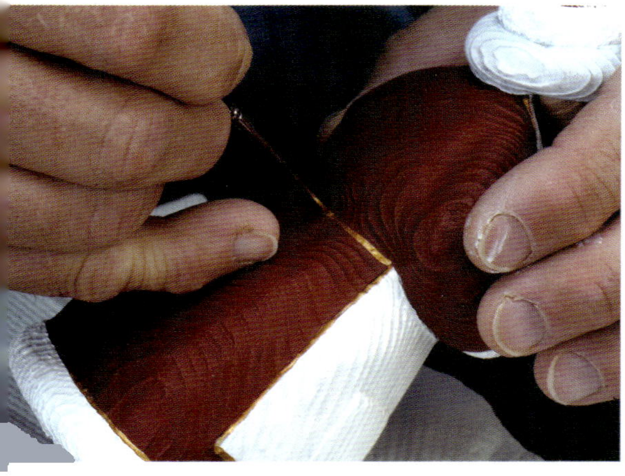

Apply apron strings in the same color as the trim around the apron.

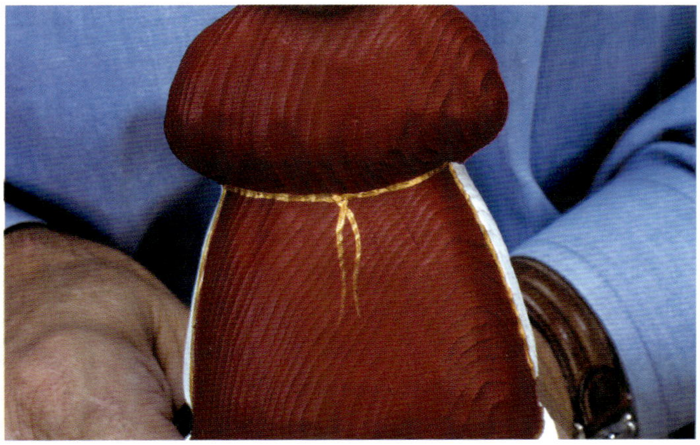

The apron strings are in place.

You may want to add a sprig of holly to the apron.

One of the last things you need to do is add the mouth (which I think is the most difficult thing you have to do). I suggest drawing the mouth with pencil, both on paper and the carving prior to applying paint. Experiment with the mouth until you are happy with it.

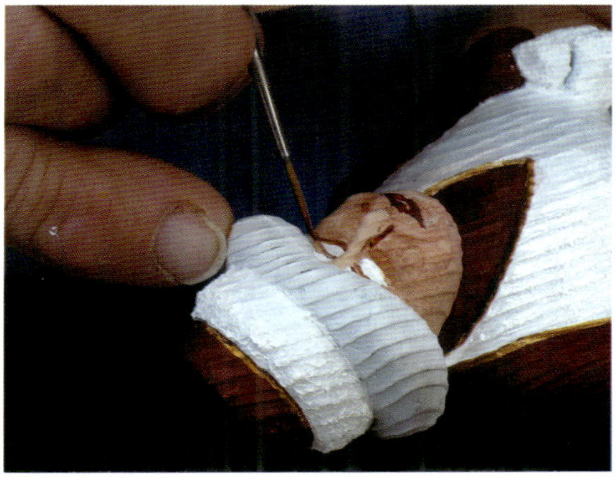

Use burnt sienna to outline the nose, the eyes, and eyebrows.

Since Mrs. Claus is going to have blue eyes, I use a dot of Cerulean blue paint with a black pupil and a white highlight to add life to the eyes. One eye is now complete.

Use a piece of 24 gauge gold craft wire to form Mrs. Claus's glasses. Use about a 1/8" shaft to wrap the wire around to create the spectacles … making sure to leave enough wire beyond for the sides. Judge the distance between each eye carefully when forming each lens.

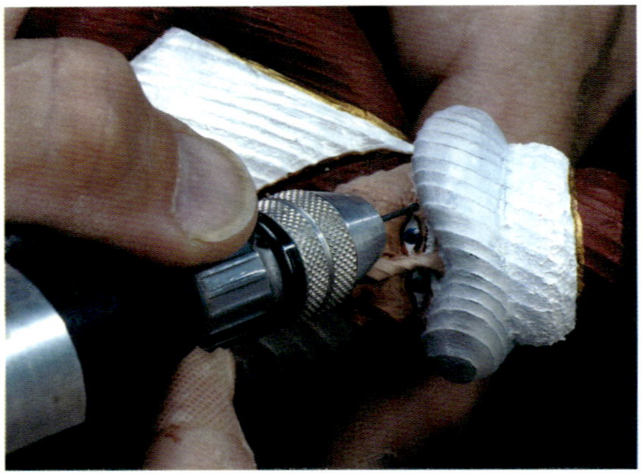

I use a small brad with the head cut off in my mini-grinder to drill holes in the sides of the head to accommodate the arms of the spectacles.

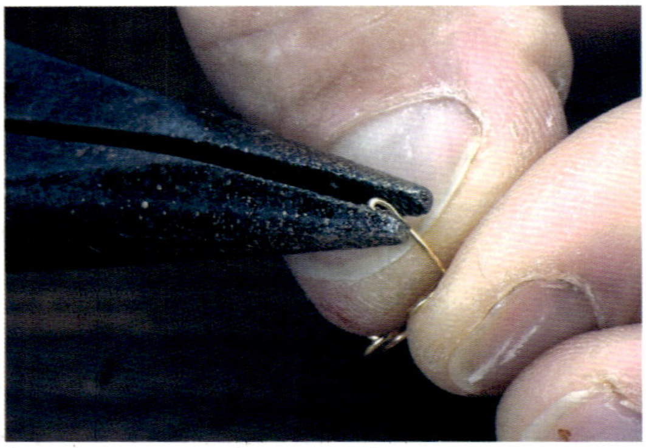

I always take my wire and double the end back on itself to make a double thickness at the end of the arm. This way the ends of the glasses will stay in place in the holes without glue.

As a finishing touch, Mrs. Claus can hold a number of things. For this project, I've decided to use a cookie tray made from brass shim stock. The cookies are made from a mixture of applesauce and cinnamon, mixed together to form a dough. They were cut out with aspic cutters from a kitchen shop and left to dry. I spray them with a fixative so they do not absorb moisture. For the tray, you can use copper or tin – or, for that matter, you can make a wooden tray. For some of my special order Mrs. Claus's, I've even made books that she has held. You can put names in these books, lists of presents, or other creative touches to personalize your figure.

The glasses are in place.

Project Two: Santa Claus

Mr. Claus has been rounded over from reference line to reference line. Redraw the bottom of the coat. I prefer to use a large, coarse carbide bit when rounding off.

Mr. Claus is considerably harder as a project, with a lot more wood to remove. Because there is so much carving to be done on this project, I use my flexible shaft grinding tool to round over from reference line to reference line and I also use a series of bits to cut in many of the details. As with Mrs. Claus, there is plenty of knife work to do. Let me emphasize that this carving can be done with the knife alone, but it is easier and quicker to use power tools. We are going to start out with the blank cut out from the front and side profile, just as we did with Mrs. Claus. Add your centerlines and reference lines as shown previously. Draw in the bottom of Santa's coat along the fur line. You may end up carving most of this line off, but I don't want you to forget this line, as it is an important one.

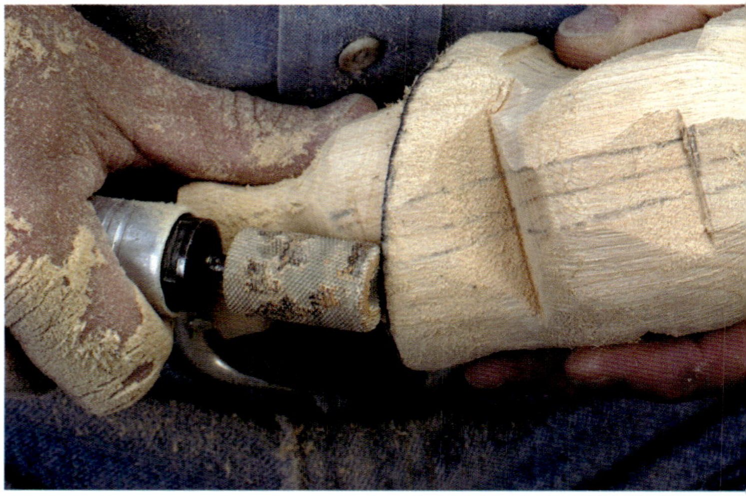

Cut in the bottom of the coat along the reference line. I'm using a smoother, finer carbide bit for this job. While you are here, round off the back of the legs as well.

As with Mrs. Claus, we've laid out the bottom of the boots and drawn the oval that will define the fur at the bottom of Santa's coat.

Draw in the fur at the bottom of Santa's coat, his belt, and one cuff.

I'm using my knife to make a V cut at the front opening at the base of Santa's coat.

Now we're cutting in the bottom of the belt and top of the fur. Use a bit you feel comfortable with for this job. You can also do this with a knife, if you prefer.

I'm opening up the coat all the way to the legs. While here, I'm rounding off the insides of the legs. You might as well round off the inside of the boot here as well … which is one of the last things we did on Mrs. Claus but it is convenient to do this now.

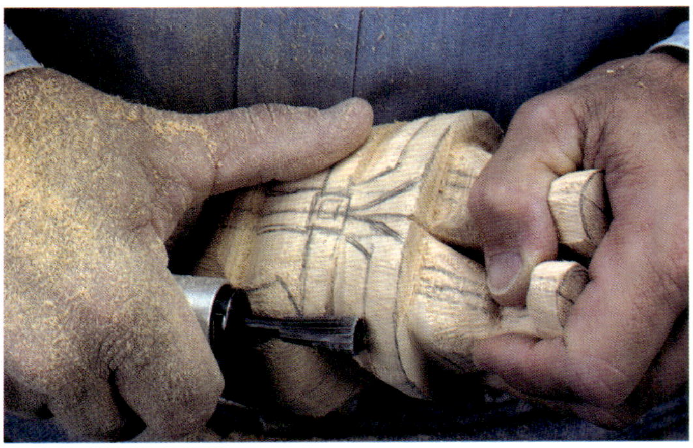

Continuing to cut in the belt and fur. Cut especially deep in the corners because we haven't finished rounding off under the arms yet.

Score the center line on the back of Santa's pants and apply a V cut to either side of the score line to round the back of the pants.

Get rid of the ridge and carve the pants down into the boots. At this point some of the reference lines on the leg can be carved away.

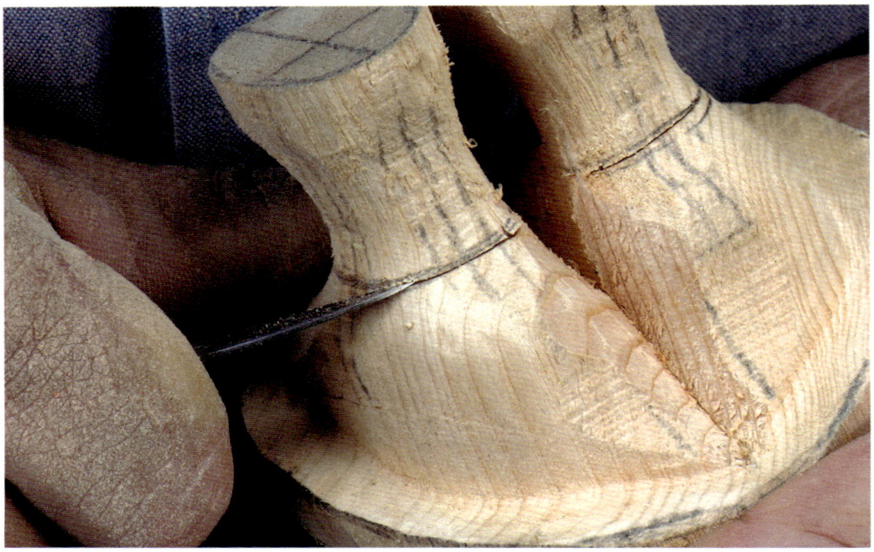

Score the line around the boots with your knife.

The legs have been rounded over.

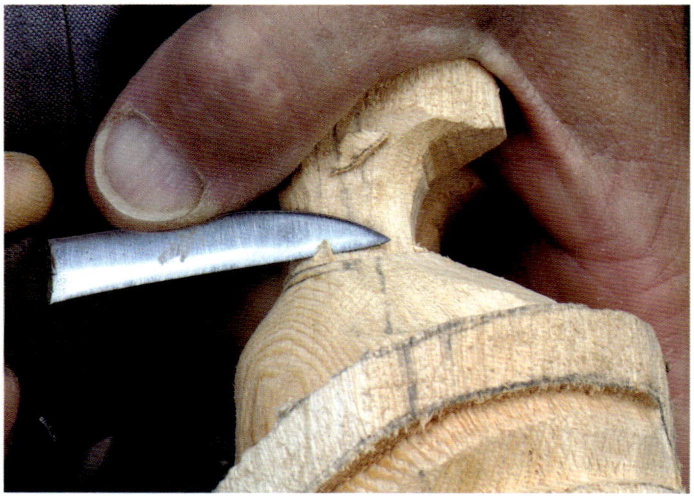

Straighten and clean the top of the boot.

Add as many reference lines to the stock as you can. Because there is so much wood in this project, it is hard to carve in any details. What we need to do is cut in the basic shapes on the body and head at this time. The cuts we make now, we are making to get rid of excess wood and give our figure some shape. Final cuts will come later.

Cut in the outline of the beard first, using either a knife or flexible shaft tool and bit.

Cut in the underside of the hat.

Now cut in the fur at the top of the hat.

Cut in the fur at the top of the coat.

Progress.

Cutting in the cuffs on the sleeves.

At this time we have cut in some of the details, but the block still remains roughly square. There is still a lot of wood that must come out to shape the body.

Cut in the arms, both inside and out.

Cutting in the inside of the arm.

I like to do some knife work to cut in the face. Begin by rounding off the face and beard into the hat. Remember to carve from reference line to reference line for the face, beard, and hair.

The face is rounded.

Cut the top of the coat into the fur.

Carve the fur at the top of the coat into the beard.

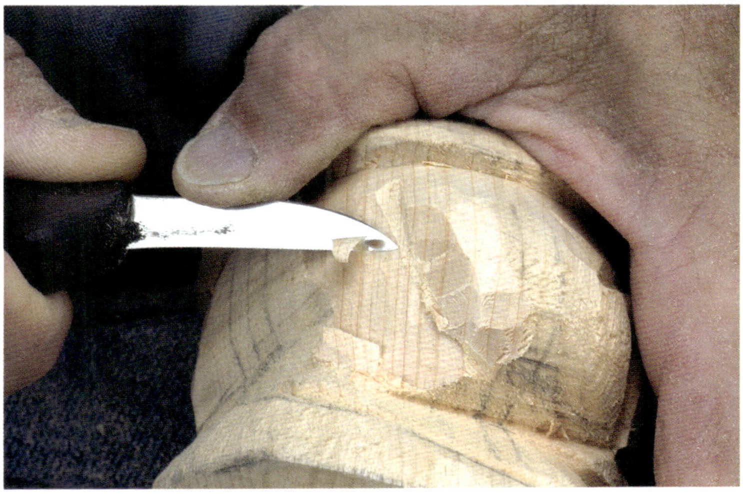

Take off some of the excess wood along the cut that separated the back of the arms from the back. Remove wood from both the back and the arms.

The fur at the top of the coat is carved into the beard.

Once again, as with Mrs. Claus, there is a lot of material in this pattern. Now that you have the basic shape cut in, you need to spend some more time rounding over the shoulders.

Start to shape the beard and hair into the fur collar.

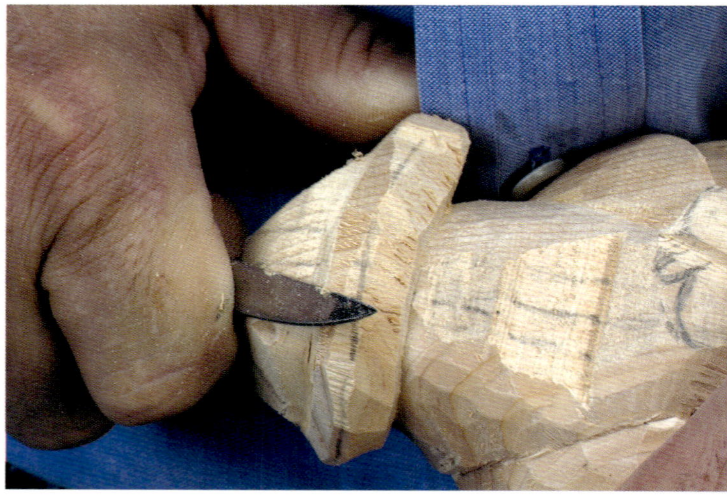

Round over the fur on the hat. You can have as much or as little fur on his cap as you wish. You have lots of material, so you can make the hat larger or smaller, as you see fit.

Shaping the hair off of the collar into the hat.

Define the top of the hat and the ball at this time.

The beard and hair are shaped.

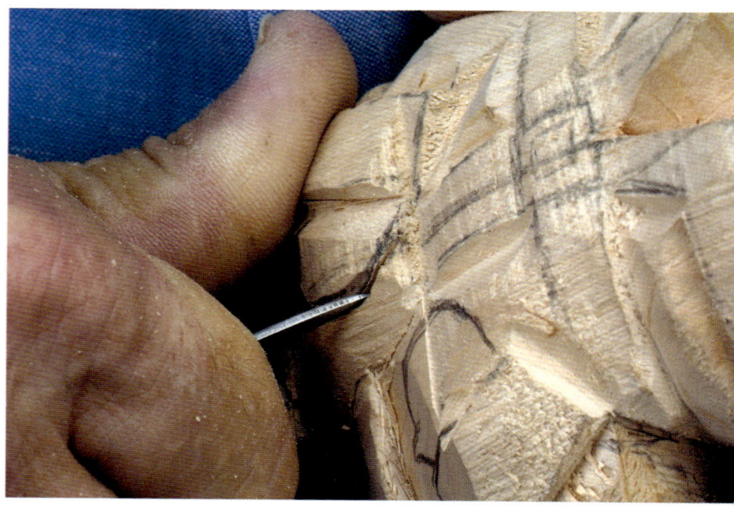

Draw in the mittens and begin to relieve some of the material from around them. Score each mitten first.

Remove the wood from around the mittens.

As you relieve both the mittens and cuffs, you will have to redefine the beard each time. There is plenty of material available for this.

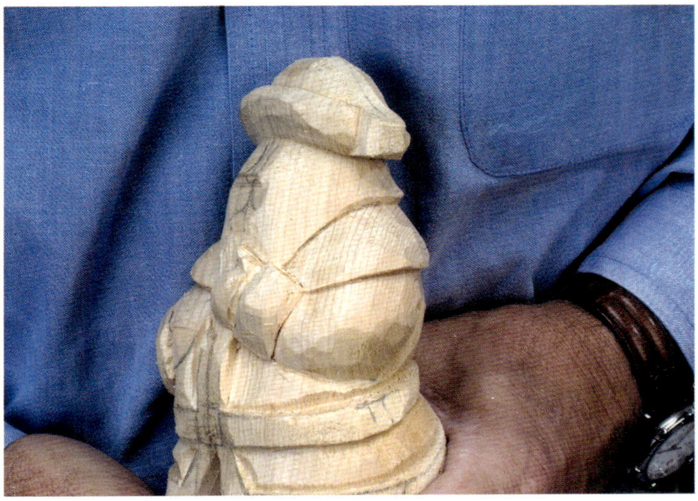

The shoulder, beard, and arm have been defined.

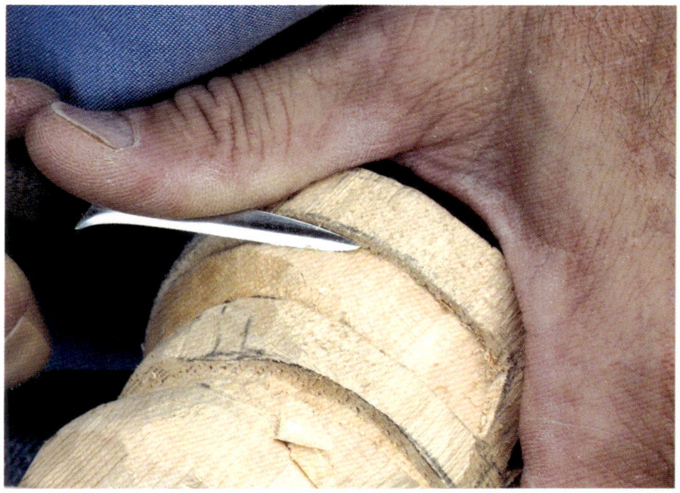

Work the area between the fur and the bottom of the belt. Clean out excess wood and ridges. This leaves the belt and fur standing up off the surface about 1/8". When you take out the material between the fur and belt, it is all right to remove the centerline. Your body may still be a little square in the corners. Take off that extra material now.

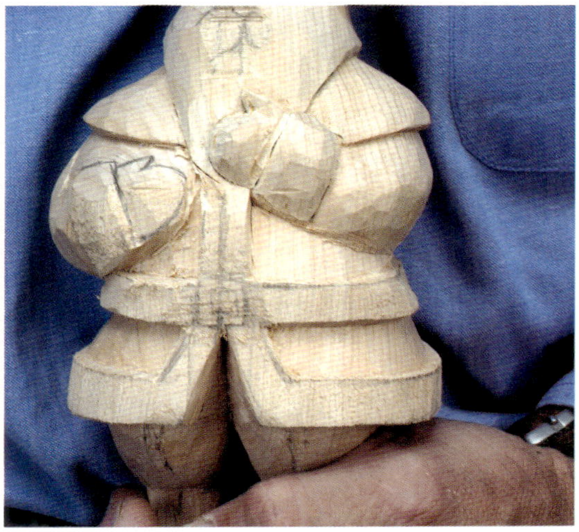

Clean up the area above the belt as well. This will help define the body.

Round over the fur on the bottom of the coat.

Define the belt and buckle. We want to leave the belt buckle higher than the belt itself. Go over the entire body rounding the belt, making sure to eliminate all high spots in corners. Remember, you need to exaggerate details so that they will survive the burning process that textures the figure. Cut away the belt on both sides of the buckle and fur, above and below the buckle.

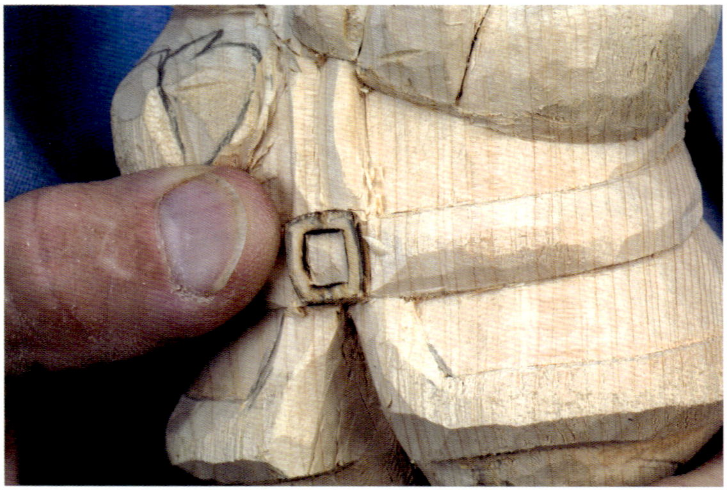

Relieve inside the buckle as well and place a V cut in the fur above the buckle to show the separation between both halves of the coat.

Continue to round off the belt around Santa's back, shaping the belt into the body.

Before shaping the arms, round over the fur collar and carve the fur collar into the back of the hair and the hair into the hat.

Earlier we rounded the legs into the fur. Now we have the fur and belt rounded into the body of the coat in the back. The fur collar and the back of the head have also been defined.

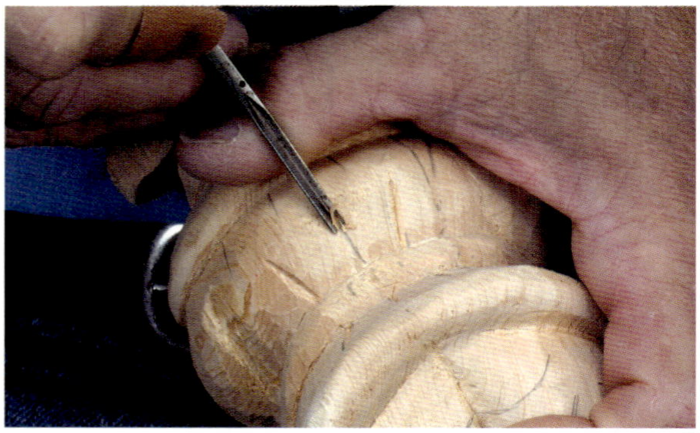

Finish up the back by adding details to the legs and creases to the coat. There are several ways to add creases to Santa's coat. With Mrs. Claus, you've seen the knife in use. For Mr. Claus, I'm using a V chisel to cut in the creases. I find a V chisel works well if you are carving with the grain. It's a little harder against the grain.

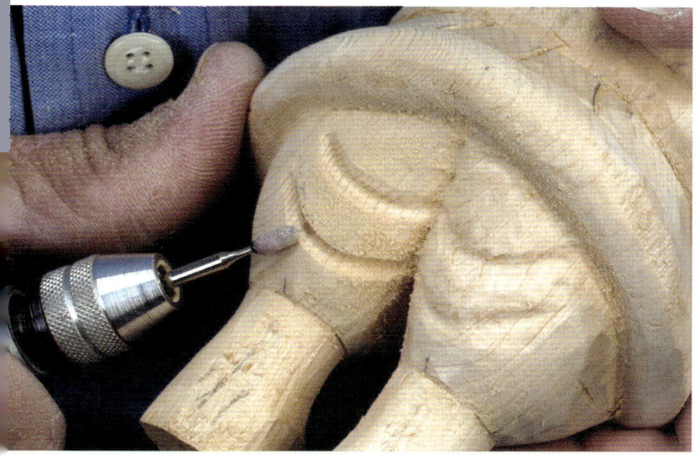

To add "creases" to the back of Santa's pants, there are a variety of tools that might be used. To add rolls to the back of the pants, I'm using my round stone on the grinder. After cutting in the crease, take the stone and round down the edges, forming some softer curves to the wrinkles.

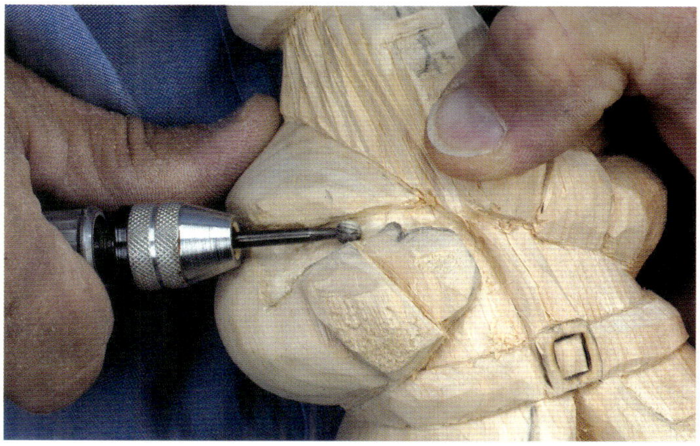

Move up and relieve the area around the mittens. There are several ways to do this. I like to use a small chisel or my mini-grinder with a round ball to cut away from the mittens and to create the indentation between the upper arm and chest.

There are a number of ways to treat the boots. In this example, I've decided to add shoe laces. First draw in a series of parallel lines from toe to boot top, then draw in a series of X's up the boots, then use a wood-burning pen to define the laces. After the boot has been painted (brown or black), I usually add gold dots at the tip of each X to represent eyelets.

Because I use such a soft wood, I like to draw the face pattern in and then use the wood-burning tool to make my initial cuts prior to carving. Feel free to change the mustache design to suit your taste.

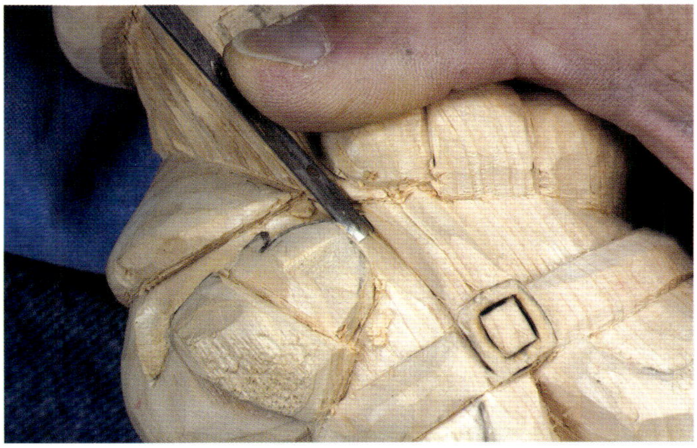

Go over your burned lines with your knife to make sure all the cuts are consistent. Relieve the underside and sides of the nose first.

Relieve from the face into the beard. Leave the mustache higher than the beard and the beard higher than the face. Round over the sharp edges of the mustache and cut in the eye as well. For this example, I used a stone to round over the cheek, inside the eye, and the beard into the face.

Cut in creases at the elbows, the belt line, and the pants. Round over and define the mittens, the belt, the fur, and the beard. At this point, your carving is finished. Remember, I've exaggerated the features because I'm going to use my propane torch to texture the figure.

Details

At this point, you are finished roughing in the features. Now is the time to round down the rough cuts and add the finishing details to Santa. Finish the hat by rounding over the rough edges and rounding over the ball. You have some choices on the end of the hat. Some people like to add a tassel or a small bell. I prefer this little ball. I use a knife to round over the ball. This is a good time to add wrinkles to the corners of the eyes as well with your woodburner. Remember, these need to be fairly deep, especially if you intend to use the torch to texture your carving. You may notice that I've also used my V chisel to cut some texture into the hair and beard.

Santa is often depicted with his bag of toys slung over his shoulder, ready for his Christmas rounds. Our Santa will be too. To make this wondrous bag, cut out the pattern; however, the pattern is merely a rough guide to follow. Each and every bag actually needs to be custom cut to fit your Santa's body. I suggest you cut your bag and form it to fit after you've finished carving. To begin, cut out a paper template first that fits the shape of Santa's shoulder and back.

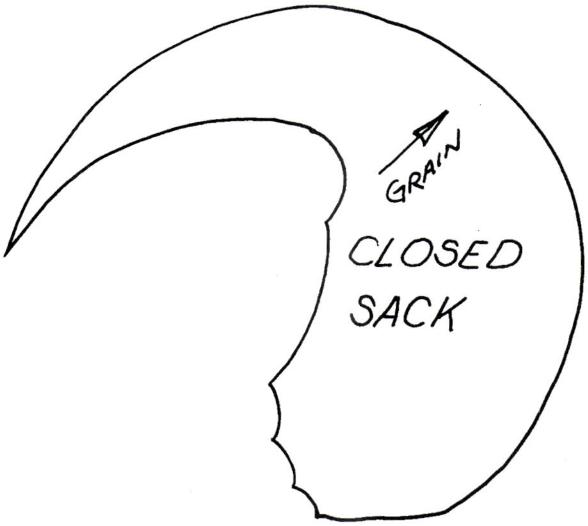

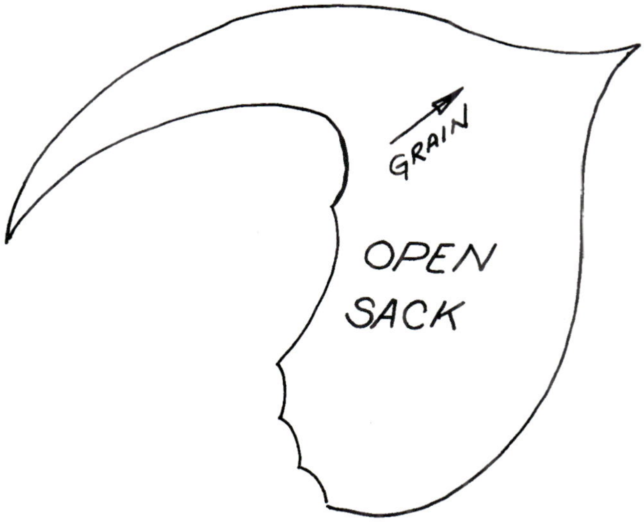

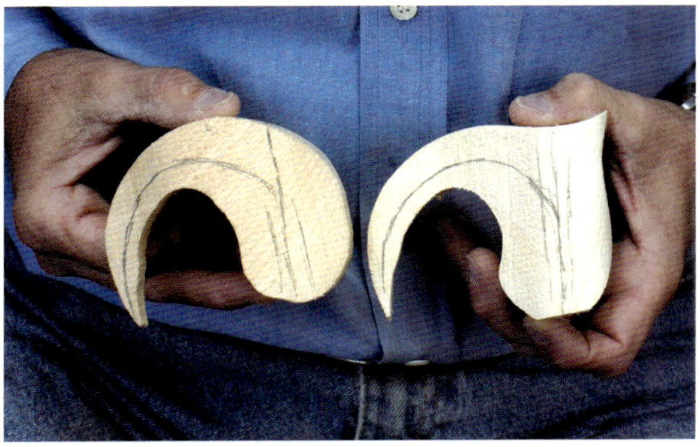

You can use either the closed or opened bag for your Santa. Cut the bag out in both profiles and add the centerlines. As with your Santa carving, round over to your centerlines. Be careful with the front of the bag, it is very fragile.

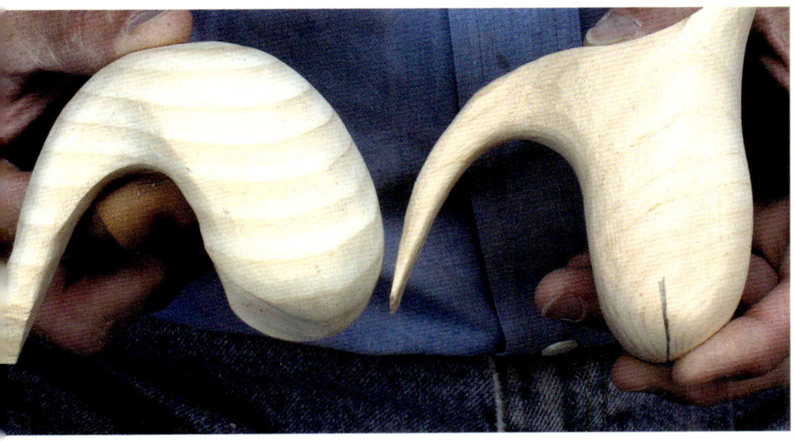

Round the bag with the tool of your choice. Make the bag as lumpy as you like. More lumps suggest more toys inside! It is at this point that things get a little tricky.

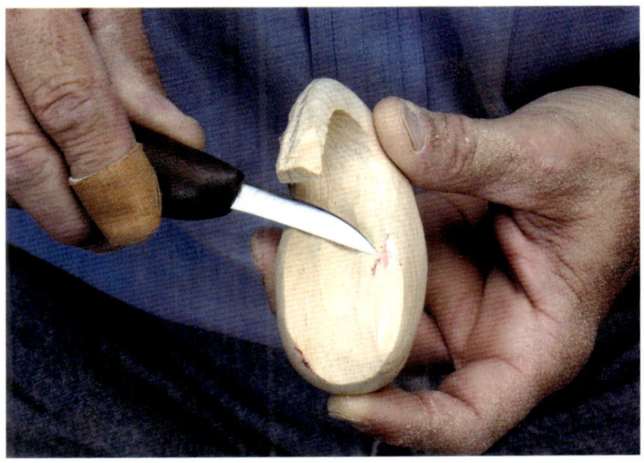

You may need to hollow out the back of the bag to make it conform to Santa's shape. I've hollowed the backs of these two examples to give you an idea what they will look like. Fitting the bag to your Santa is a trial-and-error process. After your bag is rough-cut and you have hollowed a portion of the back, put the bag away until your first coat of red gesso paint is applied to Santa's coat. (I find fitting the bag to his coat a lot easier if I have some reference marks to go by. You can try to fit the bag before you paint him, but it is a little harder.) Once the red gesso is in place, push the bag against Santa's back. Wherever red gesso marks the bag is where wood needs to be cut away.

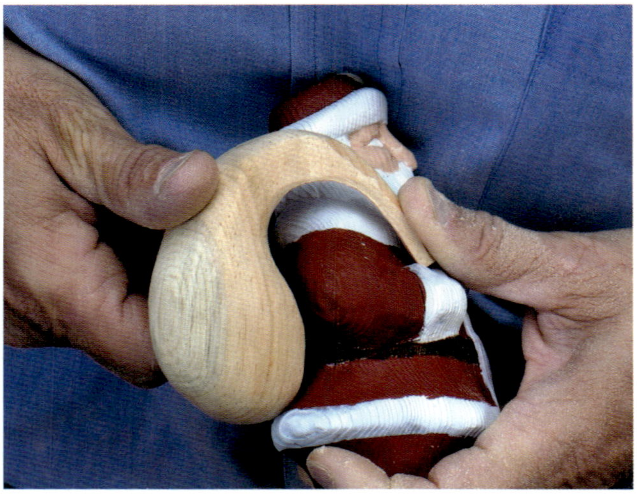

Continue reducing the back of the bag until it fits. You may have to do some work on the underside of the front of the bag that drapes over Santa's shoulder. For this operation I like to use a scoop knife, chisel, or flexible shaft. After the bag has been textured with the burning torch (along with Santa), cleaned, and sealed with sanding sealer, you are ready to paint. For this particular bag I first applied Ultramarine blue (which will appear much darker on the bag). For the second coat, I used one coat of Prussian blue with gold stars (you could use white stars as well). The bag does not have to be blue. It can be any color you wish.

Texturing and Painting Santa Claus

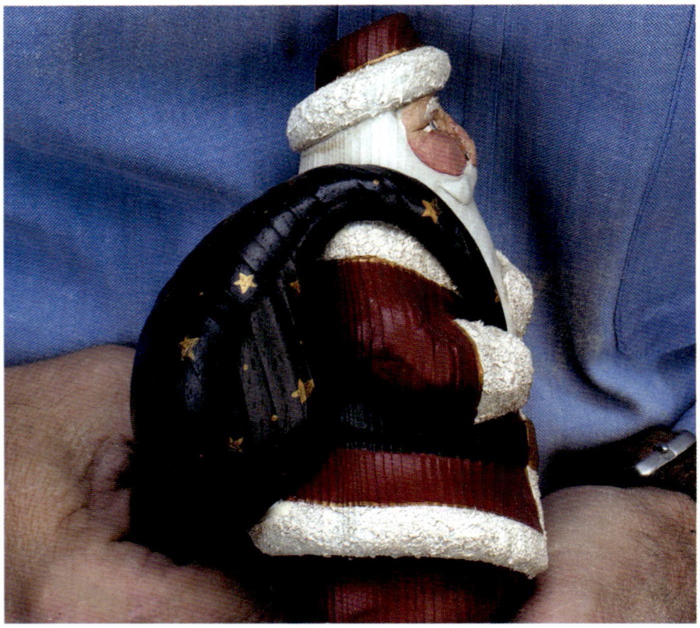

Use the torch, clean the figure, and use sanding sealer, just as we did with Mrs. Claus. When using the torch, be very careful around the face. When I'm burning this figure, I like to use a putty knife to cover the nose so I don't burn off too much detail. Keep your burn consistent throughout the entire project. Clean the face with a toothbrush and the rest of the body with a scrubbing pad. If you want to add more texture, use a very soft wire brush and clean the body with the grain. As with Mrs. Claus, seal the body with a good lacquer sanding sealer. Once Santa is sealed and dried, I spray paint the entire body white because there is so much white fur and beard. As with Mrs. Claus, I use Alizarine Crimson gesso for the suit and hat, black or brown for the belt and boots, Cerulian blue for the eyes, and flesh tones for the face. You can find all those colors and applications in the painting of Mrs. Claus. You can outline the fur with gold and use texture paint on the fur.

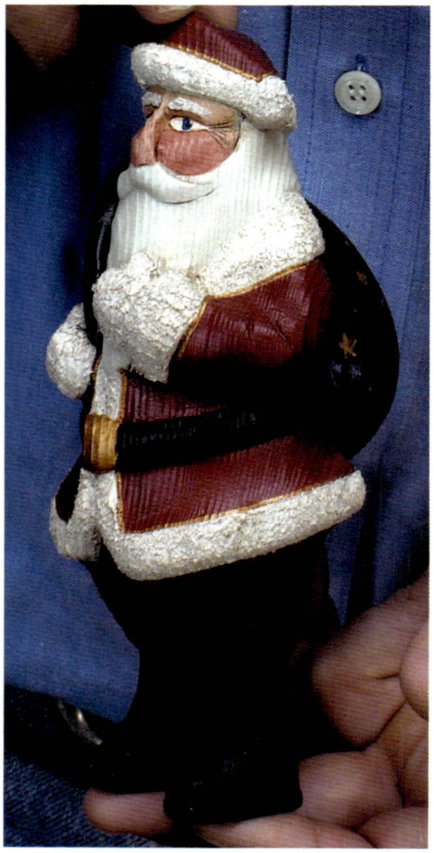

To tone down the paint on all my carvings, I use a dark oil-based stain, applied with a brush. Once applied, I pat it with a soft cloth and then take a large, dry brush and clean the figure until I reach the desired effect. As the dry brush becomes loaded with stain, I brush it across a dry cloth to clean it before continuing to brush down the figure. I continue with this technique until I achieve the desired look.

Gallery